Praise for
Thrive Solo

"Thank you to Lucy for giving the modern single woman the space to be heard for who she really is, and not who society and the press think she is – or should be."

— **Jody Day**, psychotherapist and author of
Living the Life Unexpected

THRIVE
SOLO

THRIVE SOLO

EMBRACING THE FREEDOM, JOY, AND OPPORTUNITY OF A SINGLE, CHILDFREE LIFE

LUCY MEGGESON

HAY HOUSE LLC
Carlsbad, California • New York City
London • Sydney • New Delhi

Copyright © 2025 by Lucy Meggeson

Published in the United States by: Hay House LLC, www.hayhouse.com®
P.O. Box 5100, Carlsbad, CA, 92018-5100

Cover design: Kathleen Lynch • *Interior design:* Nick C. Welch

All rights reserved. No part of this book may be reproduced by any mechanical, photographic, or electronic process, or in the form of a phonographic recording; nor may it be stored in a retrieval system, transmitted, or otherwise be copied for public or private use—other than for "fair use" as brief quotations embodied in articles and reviews—without prior written permission of the publisher.

The author of this book does not dispense medical advice or prescribe the use of any technique as a form of treatment for physical, emotional, or medical problems without the advice of a physician, either directly or indirectly. The intent of the author is only to offer information of a general nature to help you in your quest for emotional, physical, and spiritual well-being. In the event you use any of the information in this book for yourself, the author and the publisher assume no responsibility for your actions.

"The Summer Day" by Mary Oliver
Reprinted by the permission of The Charlotte Sheedy Literary Agency as agent for the author. Copyright © 1990, 2006, 2008, 2017 by Mary Oliver with permission of Bill Reichblum

First published in the United Kingdom by Green Tree in June 2025
ISBN: 978-1-3994-1643-6

**Cataloging-in-Publication Data is on file
at the Library of Congress**

Tradepaper ISBN: 978-1-4019-9911-7
E-book ISBN: 978-1-4019-9912-4
Audiobook ISBN: 978-1-4019-9913-1
10 9 8 7 6 5 4 3 2 1
1st edition, June 2025

Printed in the United States of America

This product uses responsibly sourced papers, including recycled materials and materials from other controlled sources.

The authorized representative in the EU for product safety and compliance is Penguin Random House Ireland, Morrison Chambers, 32 Nassau Street, Dublin D02 YH68, Ireland. https://eu-contact.penguin.ie

For my niece, Blue. May she know that whether or not she gets married and has children, she is enough – worthy and complete exactly as she is. The most brilliant, funny, wise niece anyone could ask for, more like a sister to me. I'm so grateful to have you in my life.

To my darling Dad: Unfathomably, it's 21 years since you've been gone – but I still think of you every day. I hope you can hear me every time I say out loud "Hey Dad. I'm still really annoyed at you for not being here! Miss you, love you." I know you're still around, especially when I see a jay flying past the window, or sitting in the tree outside my flat. Can you believe that your daughter is a published author?! I hope this makes you proud. I'm damn sure it'll make you smile. See you when I see you.

CONTENTS

Introduction		1
Chapter 1	Freedom	17
Chapter 2	Living Alone	33
Chapter 3	Solitude	51
Chapter 4	Careers and Financial Independence	71
Chapter 5	Solo Travel	89
Chapter 6	Not Having Kids	105
Chapter 7	Sex	133
Chapter 8	Friendships and Other Relationships	155
Concluding Thoughts and Eight Practical Tips		175
Endnotes		195
Acknowledgments		205
About the Author		207

INTRODUCTION

There are plenty of books out there for single women. And there are plenty of books out there for women without children, too. Books about how to find love, how to un-single oneself, how to cope with wanting kids but not being able to have them . . . the list goes on. But a book actually celebrating the double whammy of life as a single and childfree woman . . . ? A book revealing what can actually be gained by not being in a relationship and not having children? Not so much. That's where I come in!

Now, just like any other path in life, I'm not saying that being single and childfree is all beer and skittles all of the time, but what I am saying is that it can be beer and skittles a considerable amount of the time, if that is the experience you choose to allow. Within the pages of this book, you will find a celebration of all the wonderful things that life as a single woman without kids affords you. Because – make no mistake – there is plenty to celebrate.

And I know this because I'm living that life. In fact, I host a podcast called *Thrive Solo* about that life. And, as the weeks and months go by, I have the privilege of discovering more and more single and childfree women who are actually loving their lives. Hidden deep beneath the weight of the stigma, the patriarchy and the incessant social narratives that we have all been conditioned to believe for way, waaaaay too long is the secret I want to share: being single and childfree gets to be awesome, too.

As the number of single and childfree people continues to grow (the US Census Bureau reports that nearly 47 per cent

THRIVE SOLO

of the US population is currently single,[1] and the Office for National Statistics reports that the number of 30-year-olds without children in England and Wales has risen from 18 per cent in 1971 to 50 per cent in 2022[2]), countless articles about singletons have been written that appear to support this changing landscape. However, many of these can feel more like lip service to this 'new' way of being in the world, rather than portraying a genuine acceptance of solo life as truly equal to its coupled counterpart. While these articles purport to sing the praises of single life, they always seem to somehow miss the mark, coming off as patronising and unconvincing in their attempts to 'play up' a life without a partner and kids. It's as though the writers of these articles haven't even convinced themselves that being single and childfree really *is* as great as being married with kids. And so there remains an undertone of disingenuity, which subsequently continues to reinforce the old ways of thinking.

You see, there remains a far more pervasive narrative and belief system in our society that favours coupledom. An insidious and damning story that sows the seeds of doubt in those of us who find ourselves alone. The conditioning can still creep back in: that we 'should' be in a relationship, we 'should' be settling down and having families. What has been neglected in this narrative is that there is an equally valid argument as to why we might choose to remain alone.

My job here, therefore – on some level, my purpose, even – is to present the case for the defence. I aim to prove, beyond reasonable doubt, that the state of being called 'happily single and childfree' is very much achievable.

It's important to point out from the beginning that I'm not trying to suggest that being single and childfree is necessarily better than being in a couple – only that it isn't worse. Because the simple truth is this: being single and childfree and being partnered with children are two different, but equal, paths. One is not better than the other. They are equal. Being alone and childfree, and being married or in a relationship with kids, are both indistinguishably deserving of the title 'Valid, Valuable, Meaningful Life Path'.

What's more (and despite what we may have been led to believe), either of these paths comes with happiness and sadness, confusion and clarity, calm and chaos – in equal measure. Getting married and having children does not suddenly render you immune to all the usual challenges and heartbreaks that are part of being human. And, by the same token, being single and childless does not automatically turn you into a gibbering, lonely, desperate wreck.

True, there are certain things that being in a relationship affords you that don't come with being single, but on the other hand there are certain things that being single affords you that don't come with being in a relationship. The point is, they're just different. It's not a competition, and there are no winners or losers – it's a tie, if you like.

And as with anything else in life, when we go down a particular path, we're going to miss out on the things that can only be found along certain other paths. But, likewise, our path consists of things that can only be experienced on our journey; if we had taken another turn, we would have missed out on all of the things that are right in front of us on this one. As the saying goes, 'You can have anything you want, but not everything you want.' It would be remiss of us as humans therefore to claim that the 'traditional' and, let's face it, expected route of marriage and babies is inherently superior. In doing so, we're disregarding the aspects of being single and childfree that could also be regarded as superior, if only people stopped to consider the realities of both.

THRIVE SOLO

The Single Norm

According to the societal narrative, we're not allowed to be single just because we are – there always has to be some explanation as to why we've 'ended up' single. But, in actual fact, there doesn't have to be a reason for our relationship status, or lack thereof; it does not require any explanation or justification. Maybe we've chosen to be single, maybe we've wound up alone, or maybe we're somewhere in the middle. Maybe we want a partner more than anything, maybe we actively don't, or maybe we're good either way. But there is a place that exists in which you are single for no other reason than: you just are single. We don't question why people are married, and it would never occur to anyone to say, 'Why are you married?' (Although there's far more reason to question why someone is married than why someone is single, in my opinion! And clearly other people are asking this question, too: between January and March 2024, 27,908 divorce applications were made in the UK alone, while 25,254 final orders were granted during the same time period.[3])

However, there is no doubt that we still have a long way to go until the world sees us as 'normal'; until a single, childfree woman will be regarded as a *true* equal to her married counterpart. The 2020 book *The Tenacity of the Couple-Norm* shows us that the 'couple norm' – the powerful and pervasive force that insists that being part of a couple is the best, most natural and most normal way of living – is still very much alive and kicking. Here, the authors present the findings from interviews conducted in the UK, Bulgaria, Norway and Portugal that looked at the legal and policy frameworks governing 'intimate life' in each of these countries. What the authors found is that despite significant changes in society over the last few decades, when it comes to gender and sexuality, the one thing that remains almost entirely unchanged is the couple norm – in other words,

Introduction

the concept that being one half of a couple is the most normal and natural way to live.[4] And the various social movements that have propelled us forwards in so many other ways have still barely scratched the surface when it comes to single people. Across all four countries mentioned above (and, let's face it, *most* countries), the expectation is that you will be a part of a couple if you want to be seen as a respectable, normal citizen, and this is demonstrated in an abundance of ways, not least how it's woven into the multitude of laws and policies that favour coupledom – and, by contrast, disempower singledom. Not to mention the fact that this 'norm' is so deeply internalised in every human being on the planet that even those of us who are more than happy being single often *still* feel the shame, the stigma and the sense of failure in our everyday lives. This 'normative unconscious', as the authors of *The Tenacity of the Couple-Norm* call it, undermines the lives of those who do not conform to it, and can even lead us to question or doubt our own thoughts, feelings and choices. For many, the yearning to be part of a couple can feel so strong that it's as though it were coming from the inside, despite the almost indisputable fact that much of the desire is coming from the societal narrative. If the ingrained expectations were removed entirely, well . . . who knows how different things might look.

It most certainly won't happen during my lifetime that every raised eyebrow, every pitying glance, every question mark over whether we're 'really' happy, and every suspicion that we're somehow dysfunctional, vanishes from the psyche of humanity – such is the nature of the unconscious and deeply rooted stigma around singlehood. As one woman I spoke to put it, the notion that coupledom is the norm is so ingrained, it's like it's been tattooed on our skins.

So, what can we do to change these outdated narratives? Drea (38, North East England) is passionate about wanting single women – and everybody else – to challenge all of the

5

THRIVE SOLO

stereotypes and constraints that have been made up by society. Kate (55, London) shared this advice, too:

> ❝ Don't let societal expectations of what a woman's life 'should' look like coerce you into not enjoying your single life. Be aware of where that's coming from, because your happy single life is not always going to please everyone! But life is too short, quite literally, to let that hold you back from sucking up every ounce of enjoyment you can out of life. This is it. As the saying goes, there is no dress rehearsal. Allow yourself to have what you want. And if someone comes along who adds something wonderful to your life, do that! But until then, let yourself really dig your single life, doing things the way YOU want to do them, and feeling good about that. Don't hold back! ❞

I do hope that we can all join these and other single, childfree women who are confidently and happily living their freedom-filled lives, regardless of the fact that, for all of us, it can sometimes feel as if we're swimming against a very strong and indefatigable tide. Because the only way to change the narrative is for us to prove to people that our lives are valid, too. We have to own our single status, not hide it away from society, by unashamedly living our lives – whether loud and proud, or simply and quietly. One by one we must show, not just tell, that in spite of what the world assumes about us 'spinsters', there is a shocking plot twist in this tale as old as time:

- Some single, childfree women are having the time of their lives.
- Some of them are building amazing careers.
- Some of them are rebuilding themselves.
- Some of them are travelling the world.

Introduction

- Some of them are discovering their self-worth.
- Some of them are thriving in their solitude.
- Some of them are working on meaningful projects that make them come alive.
- Some of them are feeling better, happier, stronger and more empowered than they've ever felt before.
- And some of them are falling more in love with themselves than they ever were as part of a couple.

About This Book

The purpose of this book is to remind you of what can be gained from living a solo life. The topics I've chosen to include reflect the themes that have come up over and over again during my work with single, childfree women for my podcast, and during the interviews I've conducted with women – in their thirties, forties, fifties, sixties and beyond – who I interviewed especially for this book.

We'll begin with a more general chapter on freedom, and then each chapter will explore a different theme, as we look at: living alone, solitude, careers and financial independence, solo travel, kids, sex and friendships. At the end of the book, you'll find some practical tips on how to actively embrace your single life. You can read it from front to back, or dip in and out of chapters that especially appeal to you. We'll use the experiences of the women I've spoken with to illustrate how and why it is possible to be content in every area of your life without the presence of either a partner or a child. I'll also include some of my own personal reflections as a single and childfree woman alongside data from recent research to anchor the anecdotal aspects of my 'investigation'.

7

THRIVE SOLO

The final chapter will then touch on practical advice for embracing your solo status. Time and time again, I have seen how the relationship we have with ourselves is the most important one of all, so you will be shown here how you can improve this *because* of your relationship status, not in spite of it.

So, read on if:

- You love being single but would appreciate some validation as you don't see your experience being spoken about or reflected in the world around you.

- You aren't yet loving being single, so would love to find some reassurance and positivity within these pages, as well as some guidance around how to enjoy being single.

- You are currently in an unhappy relationship but are too afraid to leave (because you've been conditioned to believe that being single is a fate worse than death), so you're searching for stories and examples of a happy single life so you can believe that this is actually possible.

- Ditto to all of the above for those of you without kids, whether by choice or circumstance.

And while I can't promise that this book will miraculously change the way you feel about solo life overnight, what I can promise is that by the time you get to the final page, you will have an altogether different take on what it means to be single and childfree.

Introduction

—A Note on the Text—

Childfree/Childless: I use the term 'childfree' (choosing to not have children) and childless (not having children through circumstance). However, as we'll discuss on p. 111, I believe that some of us (myself included) find ourselves in a more nuanced situation somewhere between the two, so I do use the terms interchangeably at times. In essence, though, I'm referring to anyone without children when I'm using either of these.

Pronouns: This book was written with anyone who identifies as a woman in mind (and if that's not you, but you are here anyway, then you are most welcome, too!). I am a straight cis woman and in my own life stories I refer to my male partners. The other women quoted throughout this book have chosen the correct pronouns to refer to their partners.

Experiences: In exploring the single and childfree world, my aim is to highlight the broad spectrum of all that being single and childfree has to offer. But we all have different challenges and privileges in life, and therefore I want to acknowledge that not everything discussed in this book will be accessible for all. For example, I'm very aware that women of my generation have been able to financially access living alone far more easily than women of younger generations, especially given the cost-of-living crisis in the UK at the time of writing. Therefore, if a topic is not accessible for you (or simply doesn't interest you!), then I do encourage you to move on to the next, where I hope you'll find something more appealing. I have tried to get as many voices into this book as possible to reflect different experiences too.

THRIVE SOLO

A (Very) Short, but Not-So-Sweet, History of Single Women

Before I tell you a bit about my own story, I thought it might be worthwhile (and amusing) to have a look at the history of the unmarried woman – that strange, suspicious and fascinating figure. Much has already been written about the history of the single woman, so I'll keep it brief here so we can dive into the celebratory stuff quicker and because, let's face it, the history of singledom for women hasn't exactly been a sexy state of affairs, has it?

Witchy Women

Back in the Late Middle Ages and Early Renaissance, it was no coincidence that the unfortunate victims of the witch-hunt fever that swept Europe in the 15th century were more often than not elderly, widowed or single women. Because . . . what else was one supposed to make of these social outliers who didn't fit neatly into the patriarchal box? These 'misfits' were far more likely to be under suspicion of colluding with the devil than those who were dutifully playing the role of wife and mother. Not to mention the fact that unmarried women were often the key suspects whenever a tragedy of the economic or marital variety went down. Unmarried women working in healing occupations, such as nurses, were often suspected of colluding with the devil when, for example, a child or mother died during childbirth. A failed harvest? Surely it must have something to do with the local spinster who was new to the community? A tad worrisome, to put it mildly.

But when you think about it, weren't 'witches' actually just women who were living life on their own terms? And wasn't the vitriol that was spewed all over them actually just the result of those women living in opposition to how the prevailing

Introduction

society thought a woman should live? Essentially, their very existence made people uncomfortable. Sound familiar? These days, women who aren't legging it down the aisle or in a long-term monogamous relationship and popping out babies are still the target of suspicion; it's just that people don't label them witches any more, *à la* 1592.

'Surplus' Women

Aside from the good old witchy woman though, let's not forget about the 'surplus' women identified by the British Census of 1851. This Victorian survey revealed that there were approximately 500,000 more women than men in Britain but – even worse – almost 2.5 million unmarried women! One proposed solution to the 'problem' of these women was to send them to the colonies rather than have them – god forbid – waste their lives away as singletons.[5]

Around this time, in 1862, British writer William Rathbone Greg published an article called 'Why Are Women Redundant?' In it he wrote: 'There is an enormous and increasing number of single women in the nation, a number quite disproportionate and quite abnormal; a number which, positively and relatively, is indicative of an unwholesome social state, and is both productive and prognostic of much wretchedness and wrong.'[6] Good ol' Willy believed that if these 'redundant' British women simply buggered off to Canada or Australia, they would balance out the deficit of single women in those colonies and – hey presto! – everyone would be happy. How very charming.

This wave of 'excess' women in the mid-19th century was soon followed by another, this time between the world wars – as revealed by the 1921 British Census. After the Great War came to an end in 1918, 1.75 million women found themselves at a loss for, well, men.

THRIVE SOLO

The 700,000 men who lost their lives in the war meant another huge deficit as far as potential husbands were concerned. In 1919, the Society for the Overseas Settlement of British Women was established as a result of this 'problem'; and during the 1920s, newspaper headlines talked of these 'superfluous' (not my word) single women who were left 'on the shelf', their dreams of marriage and babies shattered.[7] Tragic and pitied, what would become of these unfortunate spinsters? Virginia Nicholson wrote of polemicist Anthony M. Ludovici in her book *Singled Out*, quoting his description of these women as 'malign . . . deficient . . . wretched'.[8] (At least none of them was forced to marry either Willy or Ant.)

So, there you have it: my whistle-stop tour of the treatment of and attitudes towards single, childless women throughout relatively recent British and European history. Fast-forward to 2024, as I write this now, and how much have these attitudes actually shifted? How much more 'acceptable' is the single, childfree woman in today's society, just over a century later?

One thing I know for sure is that the remnants of those historic attitudes remain, as the unmarried and childfree women of today are – to a greater or lesser extent – still pitied. Not to mention that they themselves, if left unchecked, still have a tendency towards feeling somehow 'less than' or having not quite 'made it'. Even the objectively neutral term 'single woman' is somehow demeaning because of the implicit assumptions around un-partnered women. And, come to think of it, the word 'un-partnered' suggests that being partnered is the default state of being for a 'normal' human.

Although it will undoubtedly take time to abolish the ingrained narrative surrounding single women, it is my hope that this investigation is a step in the right direction; and with every person who reads it, another step will be taken. I'm also

Introduction

hopeful that by having these conversations, I and others are doing our bit for women in generations to come who might subsequently suffer the stigma slightly less than we do. And I'm optimistic that my words will shine a light on the world's best-kept secret: that some of us – many of us – are single, childfree . . . and loving it.

A Little about Me

So, why should I be the person to write this book? Let me tell you a little about myself to assure you that I'm the woman for the job.

My name is Lucy. I'm 48 years old and I live in a leafy area of South West London with my beloved cat, Johnny Depp. I'm a Dorset girl born and bred, the middle child between an older sister and a younger brother – my two favourite people on the planet. My mum still lives in Dorset, and my dad died almost 20 years ago. A psychology graduate, I'm a music-obsessed BBC Radio 2 producer-turned-one-time-detective (don't ask – hated it)-turned-barista-turned-podcaster.

Aside from these introductory details, the first thing you need to know about me is that I'm very happily living my life as a single (for the past seven years), childfree woman. In fact, I feel better about myself and my life now than I have at any other stage during my 48 trips around the sun. I live, by and large, a contented, fulfilling life with friends and family who love me. I find joy in the simple, everyday things, such as walking by the river, listening to a podcast or hanging out with my cat. I feel no sense of lack and no desperate desire or need to couple up anytime soon, if ever. It's not that I'm against the idea of meeting someone somewhere down the line, but I know that I will be more than fine regardless of whether or not the right person wanders into my life next week, or in eight months, or

THRIVE SOLO

in 17 years. They will have to be really something for me to consider sacrificing my single life, though. And I use the word 'sacrifice' very deliberately, because it would be a sacrifice.

The second thing you need to know about me is that I haven't always felt this way about my single status. I have felt, and thought, all of the single-lady clichés a thousand times over: I'm a failure; there's something wrong with me; I haven't 'made it' in life because I'm not married with kids. I've had moments of such stark emptiness and loneliness that I wanted to crawl out of my own skin, such was the discomfort of being me. I don't tell you this for any reason other than to demonstrate the huge contrast between where I was and where I am now. Let me share my story with you.

A few years ago, on a beautiful July evening, I had what can only be described as an epiphany while sitting on a bench outside my flat. I was catching up on messages in a WhatsApp group with a few of my closest friends, all of whom are married with kids. Scrolling through the messages about their families – something I found, and still find, hard to relate to given my life situation – I remember thinking how surprising it was that rather than feeling any sense of lack, envy or failure, what I actually felt was a sense of relief at my single, childfree status.

I had no need to be thinking about the meal I would provide for my partner and kids that evening, and neither was I required to fashion a children's costume (how do people even do that?!) for my son's 'action hero day' at school later that week. But more than this, I had a real feeling of excitement and joy that I wasn't married or a mother. I would even go so far as to say that I felt a smug satisfaction with my life, the freedom of which means I don't spend my time worrying about picking up [enter child's name] from wherever-it-may-be or attempting to help my 11-year-old with fractions for their maths homework (which I didn't even understand when I was 11). The fact was, essentially, I realised I had free rein to do whatever the hell

Introduction

I liked, and the sense of my own independence and liberty was palpable.

That said, perhaps there was a slight sense of sadness that the lives of my friends had gone in such a wildly different direction from mine, but that was more to do with grieving the changing dynamic in a friendship group than it was wishing my life looked the same as theirs. It occurred to me that I felt happy and content, and had done for quite some time now, for no other reason than I just did. There was nothing particularly special going on in my life, certainly no whiff of a relationship on the scene, and nothing evident from the outside to explain this inner peace, aside from simply feeling good about, well, me. Why had it taken me so long to recognise this?

At that moment, and seemingly out of the clear blue sky, a thought popped into my head that I should further explore the topic of being single and childfree – not just *being* those things, but *loving* them. It also struck me in that same moment that it not only seemed crazy, but also untrue and unjust (certainly in my case and, I suspected, in the case of others like me) that the thoughts and assumptions around single, childfree women were nearly always negative. I felt an overwhelming urge to shout from the rooftops, 'World, you've got it wrong! We're not sad, lonely, desperate, unattractive, dysfunctional weirdos. And neither are we living meaningless, purposeless, loveless lives. My life is none of those things!'

My thoughts that day were ones of genuine confusion, too. Why was my life experience not acknowledged? And why was there always this question mark hanging over the authenticity of my own happiness? A fire had been lit inside me to find other women in my position – surely they must be out there? And so my podcast, *Thrive Solo* (formerly *Spinsterhood Reimagined*), was born (and swiftly followed by my membership community, Thrive Solo) with the main premise of helping single, childfree women feel better about their lives.

THRIVE SOLO

I'm qualified to write a book that celebrates single life because I have been on both sides of the fence. I've been single and miserable, and I've been single and happy. I've also been coupled up and miserable, and I've been coupled up and happy. And I know that if I can transition from the place I once used to inhabit to the place I find myself today, then you can too. I'm also your girl because every word I write in this book about the many joys, benefits and freedoms of single life comes from a place of absolute honesty and authenticity.

So, without further ado, let's dive in.

1

FREEDOM

'I've always needed to be able to move freely.
It's the way I'm built.'

— KATE (55, LONDON)

On a walk in a local park recently, I came across a herd of deer – always an incredible sight, no matter how often I see them. The herd was made up mostly of stags; only a few does lay at the feet of these magnificent beasts in all their antler-adorned glory. As I watched them roaming wild in their natural habitat, it struck me that the reason these animals seemed so at ease – at peace – was because they were moving through their world freely. They were the polar opposite of the (also polar) bear I had watched in horror at London Zoo years before, pacing up and down in its tiny enclosure as if it had gone mad. Which it probably had.

Animals require freedom in order to live a truly happy existence – and the same goes for us humans. Our desire for freedom is right up there with our need for belonging, a strange juxtaposition of the two values we crave above almost anything else. We all want to belong, but we all yearn to be free. The reality is that belonging to a relationship, and/or having children that belong to you, compromises the freedom part of that equation. When it comes to experiencing the wonder of all our planet has to offer, the freedom implicit in being both

THRIVE SOLO

single and childfree is unmatched, no matter how free one's relationship or how adaptable one's children might be.

Why is it that nobody seems to be talking about this more? It's almost as if the intoxicating freedom of a single, childfree life is deliberately being kept a secret. Perhaps if we let too many people know how awesome it is over here, all the coupled people would stage a mass exit from their lives? My own sense of freedom has a profound impact on my happiness, and I am far from the only one.

In fact, research has shown a strong correlation between freedom and our happiness and well-being. One US study in 2000 found that the people who said they felt either 'completely free' or 'very free' were twice as likely to say that they were happy about their lives.[1] But even more significant than a correlation between freedom and happiness is the research that suggests freedom actually *causes* happiness. A 1976 experiment in a Connecticut nursing home gave residents on one floor the freedom to decide, among other things, which night of the week would be their 'movie night', as well as the freedom to choose and care for a plant. On another floor of the same nursing home, the residents were not given these choices and responsibilities. Residents in the first group (who were initially no healthier or happier than those in the second group) reported 'significantly greater increases in happiness' than the other group; they were also more active, more alert, and showed better mood. Eighteen months later, they were still doing better, and their mortality rates had even reduced compared to the residents on the other floor.[2]

And speaking of happiness, studies have also found that autonomy, a key component of freedom, is the number-one contributor to happiness. Angus Campbell, a psychologist at the University of Michigan, studied happiness and published his findings in his 1981 book, *The Sense of Well-Being in America*. He wrote that having 'a strong sense of controlling one's life is

Freedom

a more dependable predictor of positive feelings of well-being than any of the objective conditions of life we have considered.'[3]

Another study on autonomy in 2020 found that people who feel they have high levels of autonomy in their lives are less impacted by issues with finance, friendships and health when it comes to their life satisfaction. And on the flip side, people who have issues with finances, friendships or health are far more negatively impacted by their lack of those things if they experience low autonomy in their lives. This study strongly suggests that the freedom to make our own decisions, without being controlled by anyone else, is far more important for our well-being than we perhaps realise.[4]

Bringing this back to the topic at hand, sociologist Elyakim Kislev's study in the *Journal of Happiness Studies* found that although both married and unmarried people who care more about 'post-materialistic' values such as freedom are happier, it's the unmarried ones who actually get more happiness out of their love of freedom.[5] In other words, us singles not only value our freedom more highly than our married counterparts, but we also get more out of it than even those married people who also value freedom highly.

There is no question that single people have more freedom in their lives, and therefore the potential to access a lot of happiness, too. This freedom came up time and time again when I spoke to different women, and interestingly in different guises. So let's explore the ways it can show up . . .

What Does Freedom Look Like?

Freedom, like anything else in life, is both a relative and subjective concept, depending on what it means to the individual. For you, as a single and childfree person, it might look like any or all of the following:

THRIVE SOLO

- Being able to travel at a moment's notice
- Being 100 per cent in control of how you spend your free time
- The ability to spend your money exactly as you wish
- Eating what you want, when you want
- The flexibility to pivot and choose an entirely different life path
- Being able to choose who you socialise with (without obligation to a partner's friends or family)
- Being able to dress like a teenager if you wish, without having an actual teenager's disapproval
- Setting your alarm at 5 a.m. without the fear of waking a grumpy partner
- The ability to be totally spontaneous without the need to 'check in' with anyone
- Full ownership of the remote control
- Decorating your home exactly as you please
- Lazy days with no one around to judge

For me, personally, freedom looks like the ability to (within reason) do what I want, when I want, and I particularly value being able to throw myself into creative endeavours uninterrupted. This chapter will take a brief look at the many and varied forms of freedom and how they benefit our single lives, and then I'll unpack some of them more fully in later chapters.

Day-to-Day Freedom

This may sound self-centred, but one of the things I love the most about being single is only having myself to consider on a

Freedom

day-to-day basis. It's bloody awesome not to have to think about anyone else when it comes to how I spend my time. My days are my own; my schedule is my own; my plans are my own; my decisions are my own; my life is my own. I'm in control of how I move through the world – or indeed if I even feel like moving through it – from one day to the next. And let me tell you, it's glorious. It's no surprise, then, that the various aspects of this everyday-kind-of-freedom were a recurring theme among my interviewees.

What We Want, When We Want

As Kate (55, London) puts it, we're able to 'move freely' and on our own terms:

> ❝ I really love having the total freedom of movement that single life gives me. I love being able to make a decision, buy a plane ticket and just go. I like being able to flow where life takes me. This is such a great pleasure in my life, and I need to be able to do it. I like my own company. I like doing what I want to do. ❞

This love of spontaneity is shared by many others, including Jess (42, London) and Cerian (39, Dijon, Spain), who was previously married. Cerian told me: 'I just like being able to do what I want when I want. If I'm going away for a weekend, I can just decide and book the flights. When I was with my ex-husband it all felt a bit like . . . "Is it OK that I'm using our money on this?" But now, everything is just for me.'

Weekends in particular can be when this freedom really comes into its own, and we're not obliged to sacrifice our valuable time doing things that simply don't interest us. Karen (51, London) spoke of this when she told me:

THRIVE SOLO

❝ My weekends are precious to me, and it's not lost on me how incredibly lucky I am to be able to do exactly what I want to do, when I want to do it. I listen to my friends talk wistfully about the days when they could spend a Saturday morning in a coffee shop reading a book, or a Sunday afternoon hunting around an antiques market with nothing but the audiobook in their headphones for company. These days, they're more likely to lament spending an entire morning being dragged around an amusement park with their husband and children, or having to make small talk at yet another kids' birthday party.

I honestly can't imagine what it would be like to have to spend my time outside of work doing activities I have no desire to do. Like it actually makes me feel anxious when I think about the hours I would have to give up for a partner and children. Does that sound selfish? Maybe. But the point is that one of *the* best things about being single and not having kids is being able to spend my free time doing the things I love and actually want to do. ❞

Personally, the thought of having to spend my weekend at Legoland or a kid's birthday party makes me want to curl up in a ball and cry, so let's not forget how damn lucky we are to have these day-to-day freedoms.

Freedom without Compromise

Then there's the freedom that comes with not having to compromise, whereby there is no requirement to give anything up in order to suit the needs of another person. Compromise for partnered people can show up in all sorts of different ways, from how they spend a Saturday morning to where they spend

Freedom

a holiday. It can even look like compromising on – or giving up entirely on – a dream they once had in order to prioritise their romantic relationship and/or children. When people follow the traditional path in life, they often brush off their own hopes and dreams, casting them aside because it's considered 'normal' to do so.

But the mental, emotional and spiritual side effects of giving up even the 'little' things can be felt deeply. Perhaps it's giving up the joy of car journeys accompanied by Bob Seger & the Silver Bullet Band because your partner can't stand them, or agreeing to give up your Saturdays to attend football matches because it means a lot to your partner, or abandoning your heart's desire to move to Montana because your partner's job means you need to stay in the UK. All of it matters.

I loved what Karen (51, London) had to say on this topic:

❝ I know that it's completely normal and acceptable to have to compromise in relationships, but I sometimes feel like people minimise how much of a big deal it can actually be. How much of ourselves we lose or let go of, and the assumption that it's always OK because 'at least we're in a relationship', and the other stuff isn't as important. But I don't necessarily agree with this because I think these things are equally important. Yes, the right romantic relationship can be incredibly important, but so are your passions, and the things you love. These are just as important as any relationship, because they're what fill YOU up; they're what enrich your soul. And yeah, they might seem small or silly or irrelevant, but are they?! I'm so grateful for my single, uncompromising life. I truly am. ❞

Many other women I spoke to also expressed their gratitude for the lack of compromise in their lives. Compromise in romantic relationships is, of course, a necessity, but the natural give and take of life with a partner inevitably means a measure of loss for both parties. For example, some people who are in a relationship may feel like they need to gain 'permission' from a partner before they decide to do, or not do, something, and that their consent needs to be taken into account. To an extent, this is part of being courteous and considerate in a relationship of course, but it can be a limiting factor – one that single people don't have to navigate.

For instance, one woman I spoke to enjoyed a gloriously free weekend during which she had her hair done, went for lunch, took part in a writing workshop and watched an old movie. She remarked how blissful it was that there was no expectation put upon her about what she should or shouldn't be doing. All of this might have been compromised if she had had to factor in a partner and their needs.

Freedom to Make the Bigger Life Decisions

Then there are the bigger decisions in life, and the freedom that being single and childfree affords us when it comes to making them. Fancy spending the summer waitressing in Rome? Go for it. Interested in trying out a nomadic working lifestyle? It's yours for the taking. Are you feeling called to finally live a life that is authentic to who you truly are? There's no one to hold you back.

Being in a position to do the things that you love and value – in my case, pivoting multiple times in my career and subsequently giving up the nine-to-five in order to pursue the kind of life that I desire – is a privilege. And it goes without saying that these things are immeasurably easier and more doable when (a) they don't directly impact anyone else's life, and (b) they don't require negotiation with, or approval from, a third party.

Freedom

Freedom to Live Where You Like

Bella DePaulo (70, Summerland, California), an expert on single life and author of *Single at Heart* and *Singled Out*,[6] told me how several years ago she was able to relocate from the east to the west of the US, thanks to the freedom her single life affords her:

> ❝ I used to work at the University of Virginia, on the East Coast. And I did what was supposed to be a one-year sabbatical in Santa Barbara, California, on the West Coast. It turned out I loved the people. I loved the university, the warmth, the fresh produce at farmers' markets – everything from the big things to the little things. I still remember walking the beach with somebody else from the University of Virginia who had moved to Santa Barbara. And I said, 'I just so wish I could stay.' And she said, 'So stay.' And with no spouse and no kids, I could. I wouldn't want to ask someone to uproot their life because I felt like doing this thing. I think it was a monumental advantage that I got to move my entire life. ❞

Both Kaitlin (42, Nashville) and Drishti (33, Mumbai) also talked about big geographical moves and how being single and childfree allowed them to do this without being limited by others' needs. For Drishti, being able to relocate from her home town in southern India to Mumbai was a truly significant event. She explains:

> ❝ I grew up in a small town in Kerala and was very much expected to marry and start a family when I was in my twenties. However, I knew that I wanted more from my life, and when a career opportunity came up all the way in Mumbai, I jumped at the chance. Had I done what was expected of me by settling down with a

husband and children, the likelihood of me following my career goals and making such a move would have been inconceivable. I'm so grateful for the freedom that being single has allowed me to have – and although this move was definitely not easy for me because of the culture I grew up in, moving so far away from my home town and family to pursue my career goals was made possible for me because of my relationship status. I cannot say the same for any of my friends. I know that many of them could only dream of such an opportunity. 🗦🗦

Drishti's story reminds us that even for single, childfree people it's not so easy to up sticks and move halfway across the country. And yet for her, not having a partner or children meant that Drishti had one less barrier to this significant life change.

Freedom to Live Authentically

Perhaps one of the most underrated benefits of having total control over the bigger decisions in life is the freedom to live authentically. By this I mean living in accordance with our own values and dreams, unencumbered by the potential pressures from a partner to live or act otherwise.

We inevitably shift, bend and change for other people, particularly when it comes to romantic relationships. As women, we've often been raised to be people-pleasers, constantly adapting ourselves and our needs to fit with those around us. Take Drea (38, North East England), who told me: 'I used to have a really hard time trying to mould myself to what other people would want me to be. I'd put on a mask for different people, and I'd be that person for that person, and this other person for this other person. [. . .] It would always be about serving them or being a better girlfriend for them.' Drea said she would

Freedom

forget about her own needs in her quest to make other people happy, which was exhausting. For the last 10 years Drea has been single, and during this time she told me she has managed to get better at being herself.

Being single gives us a golden opportunity to live unapologetically in a way that reflects our true nature. We get to decide how we show up in the world. Ileana (38, Northern California) says being single allows her 'the space to be my full self, so that I don't have to be in situations or relationships in which I'm expected to squash a part of myself.' This is no mean feat. Gina Fattore, a successful producer and writer on popular TV shows such as *Dawson's Creek, Gilmore Girls* and *Californication*, told me that 'being authentic to yourself and how you want to live your life is actually a big accomplishment.' And, no doubt, one that's easier to realise without a partner or children to consider.

And finally, when asked what she most enjoys about being single, Bella DePaulo told me:

❝ I think it's authenticity. That if [being single is] what you really want, you are getting to live the life that best suits you. And that's so important. It's kind of like, you know, when queer people felt like they had to pretend to be heterosexual, and maybe they were good at it, but it was never gonna be truly fulfilling to live a life that [didn't reflect] who they really were. And I think that it's the same thing for people who are single and want to be single; people who don't want kids and don't have them. That they are getting to lead their most authentic life, their most fulfilling and meaningful life. And I think what a lot of people don't realise, and this is one of the key points of my *Single at Heart* book: that for people who are single and really want to be, they are flourishing. Not in spite of being single, but because of it. ❞

As Bella so rightly says, it's often thanks to being single that we have the opportunity to really thrive in our lives as the people we are meant to be.

The Selfish Myth

I would like to address here one of the most common (and offensive) narratives around single, childfree women today. It was alarming how many of the women I spoke to felt the need to 'justify' their position in life by pointing out that it might seem 'selfish'. But why? Why do single women feel compelled to undermine their freedom with the word 'selfish'? Well . . . it's likely because the world has been telling them this repeatedly for centuries, and it has to be one of the most puzzling – and infuriating – connotations that has come to be associated with single, childless women.

As a result, many women feel obliged to give a nod to their so-called selfishness and then to simply tolerate the inevitable intakes of breath that can be heard when we admit to liking something as outrageous as being able to do what we want, when we want. Never mind that our freedom simply comes as a happy by-product of singlehood, and we shouldn't bloody well have to apologise for it. It's not as though we're walking around the planet being deliberately selfish, shoving mums and babies out of the way, prams flying as we push past them on our way to fulfil our every whim. It's also not that we're deliberately living our lives in a self-centred way. It's just that by default, we only have ourselves to worry about and so as a result, we can march to the beat of our own drums more than most.

And besides, the truth is that when you have an abundance of time to spend doing the things you enjoy and that make you feel good, you subsequently often show up as a far better human for the people you love. So in many ways, being 'selfish' is perhaps the most selfless thing you can do for the people in your life. When you spend time doing things that give you energy and joy, you bring that energy and joy with you into your day, and like a ripple it touches all of the people you come into contact with. When our cup is full, we're far better equipped to help fill the cups of our friends, family and colleagues too. It's the same principle as putting on our own life jacket and oxygen mask first so that we're then in a position to help other people.

In my own life, the morning routine that I prioritise is the equivalent of putting on my life jacket and oxygen mask first. When I take that time for myself each day, the knock-on effects are profound because I'm coming from a place of strength and power. I usually get up at 5 a.m., listen to my affirmations while making and drinking coffee, and do a breathwork session and a meditation, followed by a workout. I'll often go for an early walk, too. If these are the practices of a selfish woman, so be it. But all of these things set me up for a great day, allowing me to show up as my best self for the people around me.

Add a partner and kids into the mix and my mornings might look more like sorting breakfast, making packed lunches and doing the school drop-off, while silently resenting my partner, who conveniently misses out on this daily circus thanks to their commute. The chances of me actually squeezing in all of my usual routines would drastically reduce and, as a result, my cup would be half empty instead of overflowing.

All of this points to the fact that maybe . . . just maybe . . . there is a tinge of envy among those who perpetuate the 'selfish' narrative? #justsaying

Freedom from History

The final type of freedom that I'd like to touch on is rooted in a historical context, because it's worth reminding ourselves that

THRIVE SOLO

women haven't always had the freedom to be alone. The choice not to marry was barely an option in the not-so-distant past, not to mention the lack of choice around who we might have been expected to spend the rest of our lives with. For centuries, and for a plethora of reasons, women were essentially forced to marry; their fate was often decided for them, regardless of whether they even liked their future husband, let alone wanted to shag him. (Shudders.) Of course, in some cultures around the world today, this is still the case.

In the Western world, you only need to go back one generation to see how choices for women have evolved. For example, Maddie (50, Bristol) told me about a conversation she had with her mum that reminded her how lucky she was and helped her to reframe her experience of being single and childless:

> ❝ I remember having a conversation with my mum a few years ago and moaning about being single. And she said, 'You could look at it as [being that] women are incredibly fortunate now that they don't have to marry. Before, you had to marry because you couldn't afford not to: you couldn't get a house; you couldn't get credit cards; you couldn't get a mortgage; you couldn't do anything independently. And it's not really that long ago that women were kind of being sold into marriage because that was the only way to get any kind of safety or status. Actually, women now have the freedom to be independent.' And I think about that a lot because that's really quite a privilege. I don't have anyone going 'What are you watching this for?', or 'Oh, you eat a lot' and all of that. Nobody's commenting on my life. Nobody really needs anything or expects anything from me. So I can choose what I do with that. ❞

Kate (55, London) is another woman who mentioned freedom in an historical context. She talked about her (and my) generation – Gen X – and how we grew up 'in the shadow of the 1950s and everything before that', seeing the very 'traditional models of partnership'. Kate told me that she 'didn't really like what I saw. I knew it wasn't for me. Women sort of having to be beholden to men. I mean, obviously that changed, but there just seemed to be a lot of compromise and not a lot of freedom for the female part of the equation. I just knew I couldn't do that. I just wasn't sure that I could function happily in that arrangement.'

And speaking of marriage, I remember in my late twenties and early thirties – around the time my friends and peers were starting to get married – how bewildered I felt by all the women who seemingly couldn't wait to take their future husband's surname. I, on the other hand, saw the concept of changing one's name more as a giving up of something pretty huge, rather than as a gaining of anything much at all. I found it baffling – and still do – that so many women are willingly abandoning, apparently with such ease, the name that has been central to their identity for their lives up to that point. I just don't get it. Because despite Meggeson not necessarily being the prettiest of surnames, I've always been quite attached to it given that it's, well, er . . . my name. And yes, back in the day it might have been the done thing to take your husband's surname, but now, in the mid-2020s, following decades of fighting against the patriarchy for the vote, for equality, to be taken seriously without having to wear a trouser suit, isn't it just a tad old-fashioned and – dare I say it? – subordinate? In 'gaining' their husband's surname, maybe women are actually losing something far more significant: their autonomy.

When we think about being single and childfree in the context of women in history, doesn't it feel worth celebrating? And doesn't it taste that much sweeter?

Final Thoughts

Whichever way you slice it, there is a beauty and a joy in the freedom that being single and childfree brings, which, quite frankly, we should be enjoying to the full. Whether your favourite flavour of freedom is eating chocolate ice cream in bed for dinner and not being judged for it, or deciding on a whim to jump on a train and go to Paris for the weekend . . . savour every minute of it. Because not everyone is lucky enough to have it.

—**Podcast Pearls**—

'It's just that freedom of completely deciding your own life.'

— Dr Ketaki Chowkhani (39, Manipal, India)

2

LIVING ALONE

'Is there anything better than living alone? No.'
— Susan (67, Toronto)

On a Friday afternoon in June 2013, I raced home from work to pick up the keys to the very first flat that I would own. In my excitement, I remember practically snatching the keys out of the estate agent's hand. I will never forget the feeling of walking through the door and placing one purple and one pink Le Creuset mini pot down on the kitchen counter – one for garlic and one for sea salt. (Ironic, given that I barely cook.) For a while I just stood there staring around in delight at the place I still call home to this day. The new environment that I stood in was, and is, a tiny studio flat, with a mezzanine level for a 'bedroom'. It may be small, but it is perfectly formed, and I have loved it ever since. And that is largely because of – not in spite of – the fact that I have lived there alone for 11 wonderful years.

Before I bought my flat, I had been living for a couple of years in the spare bedroom of a house belonging to one of my best friends, Claire. Over dinner one night, she had very kindly invited me to live at her place while I got myself sorted after a break-up and, grateful though I was, I remember leaving that night thinking, 'There's no way I'm moving to Richmond. It's bloody miles away.' This was the girl who had grown accustomed to the 94 London bus route that dropped her off bang outside her flat in Shepherd's Bush and took her pretty much

33

THRIVE SOLO

anywhere she needed to get to in London: my sister's house, Oxford Street, work, Soho. In addition, I could run to and from Hyde Park, which at the time was important to me.

Despite my initial reaction to Claire's kind offer, I moved into her home about two months later, having seen sense (and having been given a good talking-to by my sister, who always manages to know what's good for me when I can't see it myself). Over the next two years, I fell madly in love with this leafy area by the river in South West London – so much so that I subsequently decided to put my roots down there with the purchase of my own flat and call it home. And home it remains, very happily so. My flat has become my haven, my sanctuary, my safe place, my peace, my independence, my security, my freedom and my joy. And living in it all by myself (except for my most recent ex-boyfriend, who used to spend a fair bit of time there) has only enhanced everything that I love about it. Even though it is small, and paying the bills on my own can be a challenge, it's mine, and that means everything.

I know I'm not the only one who finds living alone joyous, so let's find out what other single ladies have to say about it. For starters, Ileana (38, Northern California), who has been single for seven years, told me:

> ❝ I didn't get to live alone until my thirties. I had always had a relationship, or a roommate, or something like that. And then somewhere in my early to mid-thirties, I actually got the opportunity. It was so magical. I was able to live in this tiny little matchbox of a place that was on somebody else's property – it was an attached studio. If I were to sit on the toilet, I could wash my hands in the sink at the same time! That's how small it was. So literally just a few steps from end to end. Really tiny, but so cosy and all mine. It was so wonderful. ❞

34

Living Alone

Producer Gina Fattore, who I mentioned in Chapter 1, said this about living alone:

❝ Having my own place . . . I didn't know it would be this meaningful to me. I've always lived alone in apartments, but in 2009 when I was 40, I bought a house. I came to this house [. . .] one day at an open house. And I think I did fall in love. Like what people would say would happen with a person. I really did think [. . .] something about this feels very right to me. I could see myself moving there. I could see this other life. ❞

Much like being single, I believe that the joy of living alone is one of the best-kept secrets in the world. Except it's not actually a secret, given that the number of single-person households is fast catching up with multi-person households. The number of adults living solo in the US has almost doubled over the last 50 years, and in fact this rise in people living alone extends across all world regions.[1] It seems that this upward trend in solo living began just over a century ago but accelerated somewhere around 1950. This was perhaps in part due to people realising and embracing the many fabulous benefits of a home all to oneself.

But isn't it funny that living alone often elicits the same expressions of pity that being single does? The default assumption is that living alone is some sort of affliction – yet another unhappy side effect of being single – rather than the delicious reality I and other women find it to be. There's a sense that it's sad to think of a woman living alone, an idea that it must be lonely and isolating, and something to be avoided at all costs. *'I mean . . . isn't it awfully quiet?'* Do you mean peaceful. . .? *'Don't you get lonely?'* Are you talking about the glorious solitude? *'Isn't it a bit sad eating alone every night?'* I take it you've not yet experienced the joys of eating sushi over the kitchen sink in order to return as quickly as possible to your latest passion

THRIVE SOLO

project? *'But wouldn't you like to cosy up to someone on the sofa?'*
Do you mean would I like to try and decide on a film that will
equally suit a forty-something woman, a fifty-something man
and six-year-old twins, Jack and Lizzie? Erm, no.

Living alone needs to be recognised for the glorious experience it is for so many of us. It should not be seen as just a
temporary state of residing until we finally get to move in
with the love of our life; a stopgap until we move into our 'real
life' home with a partner, children and a dog. Living alone is
actually awesome. But rather than just taking my word for it,
let's hear from some other women, too.

The Home as a Sanctuary

One of the words that came up time and again when discussing living alone with other women was the word 'sanctuary'
in relation to their home. There were other words, of course –
haven, safe place, happy place, refuge – but sanctuary was the
most common (and it's also the one that I tend to use when
referring to my own home).

A sanctuary, according to the *Collins Dictionary*, is 'a place
where birds or animals are protected and allowed to live freely',
or 'a place where people who are in danger from other people
can go to be safe'. Now while I'm not suggesting that we're
legging it into our solo homes while being chased by baddies
or that we're 'birds' (no matter how common the British 'pet
name' for girls might be!), the words 'freely' and 'safe' resonated
with so many of us.

Jess (42, London) had this to say about her own home:

❝ It's just that feeling of, you know, I come home, and
this is my sanctuary. I've built this, and it's all me. I just
love it. I moved into this particular home three days
before the first national lockdown. And that whole

moment was taken away from me because I was literally thrown the keys at six feet apart. But once I got out of the whole lockdown thing, it suddenly dawned on me that this was my first proper home. And it was just a moment for me where I thought 'This is mine. This is absolutely my home.' I keep saying the word, but it's a sanctuary. It's comfort. It's whatever I want it to be. 🎵🎵

For me, one of the most fabulous things about living alone is being able to do what the actual hell you like within it. Going back to the *Collins Dictionary* – and those animals and birds 'living freely' – well, this is really a no-brainer. A home of our own allows us to live unapologetically freely in the physical sense, with no need to worry ourselves with the wants and needs of somebody else, or our wants and needs in relation to them.

When living alone, your home is always exactly as you left it when you return, and every single thing that adorns the walls, shelves and surfaces is there because you intentionally put it there. You can cook what you want, when you want; you can listen to music or a podcast when you want, and you can be in silence when you want. You truly can, if you want, dance around the kitchen using a wine bottle as a microphone, listening to 'This Is Me' from *The Greatest Showman*, and there's no one there to judge you. We are free to enjoy all manner of marvellous things in the privacy of our own physical space. Here are a few ideas to get you going. You can:

- stand over the kitchen sink in your pants while devouring a bag of popcorn for dinner with no one there to judge you;
- spend an entire weekend working furiously on a project that has become your latest passion and obsession;

THRIVE SOLO

- stay up until 4 a.m. so immersed in a TV series that you don't even notice that those birds I keep referring to have started singing;

- sleep until noon on the weekend, resting easy in the knowledge that there is no tiny human that needs transporting to a birthday party, or god forbid, a party where you're actually expected to stay for three hours and make small talk with other parents;

- stay in on a Saturday night in blissful solitude (more on solitude in Chapter 3), reading a book, having a long bath or watching a film, rather than having to begrudgingly accompany your partner to dinner with their parents (both of whom make you want to take the fork at the fancy restaurant and shove it in your eye).

These are just a few of the endless examples I could give you that attest to the fabulousness of living in a sanctuary all of your own. You're welcome.

Bella DePaulo (70, Summerland, California), who we met on p. 25, spoke of the freedom to go about her day either 'in utter silence, with no one chatting to me, no TV, no music, no nothing' or 'with music or the TV on, or talking to someone'. She told me that when she's at home, she loves getting to decide exactly what fits her mood and her schedule, which, for her, can sometimes look like 'staying up until five in the morning, and sleeping throughout most of the morning'. Bella also spoke of the 'unselfconsciousness' of living on her own, meaning she's able to 'think with my whole mind and feel with my whole heart. Whenever somebody else is around, even if they're just quietly going about doing their own thing, there's a piece of my attention that's devoted to them, whether I want it to be or not.'

I also asked some of the wonderful women inside my Thrive Solo membership about their thoughts on living alone. Here's what they relish about being able to fully embrace being themselves in their own space:

- Jo (55, Cardiff) loves 'dancing madly' whenever she feels like it.

- Gemma (44, East Sussex) enjoys having dedicated 'space for making art and space for meditation'.

- Pip (39, Isle of Wight) likes that she doesn't 'feel obligated to be or act a certain way' at home, and she enjoys that 'the dogs sleep on my bed if they want to, and I love that.' Pip also says that she 'can have my music on as loud as I want in the morning to do my workout in the living room, and I can work on photography and video projects in peace'.

- Lindsay (43, Royal Leamington Spa) appreciates being able to 'leave my place in a mess and [that] no one will judge; I also don't have to clean up after anyone else. I feel complete and utter freedom to do what the hell I want because no one is watching me. Solo life is bloody awesome!'

Eating habits were also a popular one within my Thrive Solo community. Philippa (37, Guildford) told me that expressing herself 'comes out in my cooking. When I've been in a relationship, I've cooked to suit the other person. But when I'm alone, I can really have fun with it and get creative in a way that I wouldn't if someone else was there.' Victoria (39, Harrogate) said that she likes 'eating when I want; I just eat when I'm hungry. I don't really have a particular time to cook dinner. I also have ice cream for breakfast sometimes, just because I can!' Lindsay (43, Royal Leamington Spa) says that 'if I want to eat breakfast for dinner, no one is there to question it', and Sophie (69, New York City) shared that 'I never, ever cook, so

THRIVE SOLO

it's a non-activity that I give myself permission not to do, as I've always loathed it.'

Jo Good, BBC radio presenter, told me that living alone is 'hugely addictive'. We laughed about the fact that we both love sleeping alone, with Jo saying that while it can be lovely to cuddle up with somebody, 'I actually wonder whether it's natural for us to go to bed with another human being every day of your life, year after year.' She added that she's never wished there was someone in her bed with her, 'whereas when I have shared beds with people, I've always thought "I wish they'd go now", but you can't beam people in and out!'

Well, you can't say fairer than that.

Peace and Quiet

A couple of months ago, I was house-sitting at my aforementioned friend Claire's house while she was away working. The house is part of a terrace of gorgeous old workers' cottages, meaning that all the gardens are attached except for the garden fences that separate them. There was a heatwave in the UK at the time, and I would spend my days working at the kitchen table with the doors wide open to the garden. On several occasions I was interrupted by the sound of screaming children (and adults) in the neighbouring gardens.

One day in particular, I found myself with stereo surround sound as the two couples on either side of me proceeded to have massive rows at exactly the same time. On one side, the wife was berating her husband for having come home late the previous night, leaving her to deal with their kids; and on the other, the husband was berating the wife who'd had the audacity to ask him twice if he could put the recycling out. 'If you've asked me to put the recycling out, then I'll put the recycling out!' I couldn't help but feel more grateful than usual for the peace and quiet that come as a happy by-product of living alone.

40

I'm not suggesting that every household that consists of a family, or a couple, or some combination of those things is living in some kind of hell; but what I am saying is that it's only when you live on your own that you know for 100 per cent certain that no one within those four walls has the power to upset you, annoy you, hassle you, shout at you, moan at you, complain at you, bore the crap out of you, or generally shift your mood from cool, calm and collected to angry, upset and frustrated. No one can come home from work in a bad mood and take it out on you, or come home from school and have a massive tantrum for two hours, and scream and shout and be rude and annoying. Or worse, ask Alexa to play 'Baby Shark' by Pinkfong for the 97th time as you silently cook fish fingers and dream about running away to a desert island. Annie (44, San Antonio, Texas) would certainly have something to say about this:

> ❝ I've been living alone for eight years; I love it. I'm very audio sensitive and so just the noises that other people make drain my energy. And then also, as an introvert, feeling tired or [that] your energy has been drained because you've been working all day, or you've just been out with friends [means that] having to come home and be polite to someone is difficult. Just having a quiet place to retreat to [after] being out in the world is so awesome. ❞

Kate (55, London) also values silence and views it as integral to her being able to replenish her energy after a long day at work:

> ❝ When I come home in the evening, especially if I'm working a lot, I really do need to just have some time by myself, not speaking, not communicating. I really need downtime to recharge [so that I can] live my best life. ❞

THRIVE SOLO

So, peace is clearly one of the most underrated benefits of living by yourself. It's one of the things that many of us crave, along with happiness. But we've become so used to celebrating the nuclear family household, and holding that up as the ideal, that we've forgotten how much there is to celebrate about the peace that comes with living alone.

Emotional Safety

Sometimes people who live alone lament the fact that they do, and that is of course totally valid. But something that perhaps doesn't get enough credit or acknowledgement is the emotional safety that comes with living alone.

When there are other people living in the same space as you, it's like being part of an ocean of waves that can suddenly sweep you off in another direction at any given time. You might be happily swimming along in your own lane, but when a 15-foot wave appears, you really have no choice but to be carried along with it. Whereas when it's just you paddling in your own little pool, you're protected from any other waves that might threaten to come along and disturb your calm waters.

An underrated advantage of living by yourself, therefore, is the knowledge that while you are behind the closed door of your own home, there is no danger that your emotional landscape can be changed or shifted by someone else's mood. It is without question one of the things that I'm personally most grateful for, especially having lived previously with several boyfriends whose mental states undoubtedly had an effect on my own. Not that there is anything at all wrong with this – it's a completely normal and natural part of living with a partner – but not having to deal directly with the feelings of someone else on a daily basis is a massive bonus.

That our homes are safe havens really *means* something. And this isn't just because of the more frivolous reasons mentioned above, such as arguments about who puts the recycling out; it's also true for some pretty serious reasons, too. For example, it is well documented that stress can have a major impact on our physical and mental health. Research shows that stress can cause a huge number of issues, from anxiety to irritability, diabetes to depression, headaches to heart disease, and mood swings to memory loss. Now, I'm not pretending that living alone doesn't come with its own set of stressors – we'll look at the financial downsides of living alone in a different chapter, and emotional loneliness is also an issue – but we *can* be grateful that the stress so many in familial households experience in the form of marital discord, struggling offspring, mental health issues, overloaded schedules, lack of 'me' time, or even squabbles around who's going to do the washing-up are not something we need to concern ourselves with.

It's interesting to note that a study done by Pennsylvania State University shows that many people find their home life – childcare and household chores – to be even more stressful than their work life. During their study, the researchers looked closely at a variety of people's levels of the stress hormone cortisol throughout their days. The participants were also asked to rate their mood, both at home and at work. The data showed that cortisol levels in both men and women were significantly lower when they were at work, compared to when they were at home.[2]

Furthermore, the study found that the female participants said they felt happier when they were at work, whereas the men felt happier when they were at home.[3] The implication from this is that women dealing with kids, a partner and household chores felt so stressed at home that they actually felt happier when they were at work.

THRIVE SOLO

All that is to say that the potential benefit of having reduced stress levels at home if you live alone is not to be sniffed at when it comes to emotional health and safety.

Bright Yellow Sofas

As I mentioned earlier, I live in a studio flat designed for a hobbit. While small, it's beautiful and it's mine. And more than that, it is literally an expression of 'me'. It's exactly what I would look like if I were to suddenly turn into a flat. Every inch of it feels like a reflection of who I am, what I love, and how I spend my time. And it turns out I'm not the only one to feel this way. Many of the women I interviewed spoke of the joy of making their space their very own and how they view their home as a reflection of who they are. For instance, Gemma (44, East Sussex) said of her home: 'It looks exactly how I want it. I've made it a space that I love being in and that I am truly grateful to have. I've decorated to suit my style and taste, and I often get told my home reflects me and my character.'

Much as I enjoyed the periods in my life when I lived with boyfriends, I distinctly remember having 'those' conversations in relation to our respective belongings. (And don't even get me started on music choice and volume, thermostat settings or sports channels.) I'm reminded of the scene in my favourite film, *When Harry Met Sally* (1989), where Jess and Marie have an argument about an infamous wagon wheel coffee table, or the big white dog in Joey and Chandler's apartment in *Friends*. The thought of having to live every day with pictures and decor that not only don't spark joy but instead spark misery brings me out in a cold sweat.

Maddie (50, Bristol) spoke of this when she told me about the statement wallpaper in her house, which is covered in green foliage and tropical yellow birds:

Living Alone

❝ I can't imagine any man I've ever come across being OK with this wallpaper! And all the knick-knacks that I've got everywhere and all the quirky stuff and it's like, yeah, cos it's me. I [sometimes] think of the home I had with my ex-partner, which was such a compromise, and he still thought that it was 'full of shit', as he charmingly put it! And it took me a really long time to feel safe enough, I suppose, and confident enough to just live in my own space and have it exactly the way I wanted, but now I can. I don't know how to put it really. It is such a luxury, I think, and it's something I am incredibly grateful for. ❞

Maddie isn't alone in going for bold statements in decor. Drea (38, North East England) bought herself 'a bright yellow sofa because it's my favourite colour and I wanted a bright yellow sofa, and so I got it!' And Bella (70, Summerland, California) said, 'I like that I can use my space any way I want to. I put my desk in the living room because in the living room I have a peek of the Pacific Ocean. It's my brightest room; it's my cheeriest room. And so, you know, why would I stick my desk somewhere else when I have full control of where I want to be and how I want to arrange it?' I couldn't agree more.

There's a more serious side, too, to our bright yellow sofas and tropical bird-adorned wallpaper. There is much research to show that our home environment has a serious impact on our mental health.[4] Some environmental factors that affect our state of mind include: aesthetics, i.e. clutter or general mess; sensory factors, i.e. noise, temperature and smells; and people, i.e. conflict and communication problems.[5] A study published in *Personality and Social Psychology Bulletin* found that women who described their living spaces as cluttered were actually more likely to be both tired and depressed than those who said their homes were restful and restorative. Moreover, the research

THRIVE SOLO

also found that those women who had described their home as cluttered had higher levels of cortisol.[6]

This seems to play out more broadly, too. Lara (51, Reading), who used to be a teacher, told me:

> ❝ When I was teaching, [my house] was often really messy because I was just too exhausted to do anything about it. These days, I'm not like that, and everything's where it should be, and I like order. I've literally just been reading something about how [. . .] ordering your outside environment can help reduce the chatter in your mind, which is very interesting. ❞

And here us singles benefit again, this time from not having to live with either a partner or children who leave dirty socks and pants on the floor, washing-up in the sink, scum in the bathtub, and general crap . . . everywhere. A peaceful and aesthetically pleasing home can cultivate a greater sense of well-being than one that is constantly cluttered and chaotic, and even such things as the colour of paint on your walls or sofa can positively or negatively affect your mood.

So there you have it. The peace and quiet of living alone doesn't just benefit us on a surface level; the science shows that reducing stress – which can often be caused by living with other people – can also positively impact our mental health.

Empowerment, Achievement and Meaning

Living alone can also create a sense of empowerment and achievement. And many women I spoke to experience this as a happy, and sometimes unexpected, by-product of having their own place.

When I asked Jess (44, London), for example, what it means to her to have her own home, she said, 'The fact that I can look

Living Alone

around and go, "I've done all of this. This is mine and there's no one here that's gonna tell me otherwise." And I feel a massive sense of pride in that.' Emma (52, London) agrees, and told me that she feels 'an achievement at having bought it on my own, and especially in London as it's so expensive! It's mine, and I'm not dependent on anyone else for it.'

Maddie (50, Bristol) shared this with me when I asked her what it feels like to have her own home:

> ❝ Oh god, it's everything. Last weekend, I went to stay with a friend. It was her birthday, and she had a bunch of people staying and it was lovely. And the next day I was so grateful to be able to drive home, and the flat was exactly the way it was when I left it. [. . .] And I feel really proud of the past 10-plus years where I've found jobs and worked really hard and got to the stage where I can support myself and was able to buy my flat. There's so much pride. And I felt so much more secure when I managed it solo. ❞

Clearly, for many women, living alone affords freedom and independence, the knowledge that you are in control of your life, and the strength of mind that comes from that.

Final Thoughts

It's been fascinating to speak to so many other women who love living alone as much as I do, despite the glaring lack of positive portrayals in the media. It was lovely to feel a sense of connection with these women, but what I learned didn't actually surprise me. Because if I'm mad about living on my own, it makes perfect sense that others would be too. And it doesn't take a crazy cat lady to see why: the peace and quiet, the clean and orderly environment, the emotional safety, the

THRIVE SOLO

opportunity to reflect who we are in every picture on the wall. Then there are the smaller things, too, like having control of the room temperature or the remote control. And the biggest gift of all: the opportunity to learn to embrace being comfortable in your own skin and explore the truest parts of yourself.

One thing I found particularly interesting was that several of the women I spoke to expressed doubt about ever living with somebody again, such was their love of living alone. This is something that I've thought about more and more recently. And while I'm not entirely closed off to the idea of a relationship in my future, the notion of sharing my space with someone brings me out in a cold sweat.

If you were in any doubt as to the multitude of benefits that come as a side effect of solo living, I sincerely hope that these last few pages have shifted your thinking, even if by just one degree. Because there is no doubt in my mind that it can be a delicious and unapologetically 'selfish' way of living, especially in a society where women so often shoulder the burden of domestic responsibility in cohabiting situations. Having a place to call your own can be truly liberating, and it's so much more than a temporary state of residing, a stopgap until we move in with someone. We singles have got this. We are smart. We are capable. We are independent. And our homes might just be the loves of our life.

I wanted to finish this chapter with a few words from Sabrina, another of my Thrive Solo members, who expressed so beautifully in one paragraph what I've taken pages and pages to explain:

> ❛❛ For as long as I can remember I've been partisan of 'a room on my own' style. Now it is my whole apartment. It reflects my worthiness. It is my nest, my safe heaven. There I am in my own rhythm, mess or tidiness. I follow my bliss without ever wondering or thinking

Living Alone

about someone else's thoughts, needs, judgements, expectations, demands or pressures. Actually there is never any pressure because I can just totally be on my own terms. I can eat what and whenever I feel like. Sleep as long as I want, wake up as often as my body needs it, and I never wonder if I'll disturb anybody. I can dance like a mad girl in my kitchen or living room, or I can meditate. I can draw, paint, write on my kitchen table and leave it as it is for days, if I want to. I can keep my secret thoughts, journalling out in the open as long as I want to. Being solo in my own space is the perfect life. **🥠🥠**

Yes indeed, Sabrina. I couldn't agree more.

—Podcast Pearls—

'Once you are truly, truly happy with where you are, and how you feel about being single, and how you feel about yourself, the bar is so high, because when you genuinely are that happy on your own, why on earth would you compromise it in any way? It's actually made it quite difficult for me to [consider changing my situation] . . . I don't really know where to go from here! And I can confidently say that if I spend my entire life on my own, I'm OK with that, because I would rather that than anybody be able to disturb my peace, or upset my life in any way, because I'm not willing to compromise on the big things.'

— Pip (39, Isle of Wight)

3

SOLITUDE

*'Solitude is a glorious, shining gift that
I need to give to myself every day.'*

— KERRI (51, BRISBANE, AUSTRALIA)

Similar to the stigma around being single, there is a stigma attached to solitude. This speaks far more to the loneliness with which it is often conflated than to its true meaning, which, by definition, represents the *joy* of being alone. This misunderstanding means that solitude is often interpreted as a negative state, as though extended alone time is inherently undesirable or unwelcome. And while, of course, there are many people who *are* lonely and find time on their own unenjoyable and even intolerable, there are also those of us who love it and subsequently delight in all of the wonderful things that intentional time alone can bring. Indeed for some of us, intentional solitude is something we prioritise and cannot do without.

I certainly fall into this latter camp. It occurred to me not so long ago that some of the best moments of my life have been during times of solitude. Of course there have been fabulous occasions in the company of friends and family, no question, but many of my most profound moments have occurred by myself. Needless to say, the various milestones of a 'traditional' life will be listed among the best times for many people – the day they got married, gave birth to a child, moved into a dream

51

THRIVE SOLO

family home, or went on a honeymoon. And while inevitably these events make up many of life's great moments, it would be remiss of us to discount those empowering, meaningful, wonderful moments that occur without witness. In some ways, these can be the most significant. For me, this has looked like sitting in meditation, a stunning sunset by the river early in the morning or a moment of flow when working on a passion project. It has truly been in these moments when I've been the most *alone* that I have felt the least lonely.

Lara (51, Reading) feels so strongly about carving out time for solitude that she blocks out alone time in her calendar and treats it as a non-negotiable appointment with herself:

> ❝ Solitude is really important to me. I read an awful lot, or I sing or play guitar and listen to music. So a lot of the time I'm not in silence in solitude, but I'm just in my own being. I can't imagine not craving solitude. If things are getting busy, then I need to ensure that I actually calendar in 'breathe'. If I see a busy week coming up, I'll just write 'breathe' for the evening, and then I'll know not to block anything else in because I really need that time to just be. ❞

Yet despite these profoundly positive personal experiences, the perception of and narrative around solitude often paints a negative picture. To unpick why, and why this view is flawed, let's briefly take a look at the data and studies around the issue.

The Science of Solitude

The theory of evolution states that human beings are social creatures who require other humans around them in order to survive; we all know that social interaction plays a significant role in our happiness and psychological well-being. Yet while I'm not questioning or challenging this truth, what I *am* doing is suggesting that spending time alone can be equally as important and beneficial for some people's well-being as spending time with others. Dr Thuy-vy Nguyen from Durham University – who studies solitude – explained in a 2023 article why solitude can be beneficial. In her series of experiments with undergraduate students, she found that anxiety dropped after just 15 minutes of being alone. And in a worldwide survey of more than 18,000 adults, she found that more than half voted for solitude as 'one of the key activities they engage in for rest'.[1]

There is other research, too, that speaks to an array of benefits that have been attributed to solitude. For instance, Christopher R. Long and James R. Averill named freedom, creativity, intimacy and spirituality among those benefits in a 2003 study.[2]

But despite these and other studies that show solitude as a positive state, the vast majority of research has looked at its negative impacts. So, just as the stigma around being single exacerbates the idea that the un-partnered are automatically less happy, the stigma around solitude does much the same. Willfully spending a lot of time alone tends to elicit the assumption that you're somehow flawed, a bit weird, and certainly not as happy as those who spend the majority of their time in company. As Sara Maitland points out in her book, *How to Be Alone*: 'we declare that personal freedom and autonomy is both a right and good, but we think anyone who exercises that freedom autonomously is "sad, mad or bad". Or all three at once.'[3]

So, even if you're someone who quite obviously relishes their alone time (like I do), in a society that places so much weight and value on relationships – familial or otherwise – you might still find yourself the victim of enquiries about why it is you seem to want to be by yourself so much. *Are you OK? Is it healthy? Aren't you lonely?* Anthony Storr talks about this in his book, *Solitude: A Return to the Self*: 'In a culture in

THRIVE SOLO

which interpersonal relationships are generally considered to provide the answer to every form of distress, it is sometimes difficult to persuade well-meaning helpers that solitude can be as therapeutic as emotional support.'[4] Mr Storr is bang on the money with this. We live in a society where there is barely any acknowledgement of the fact that solitude can be just as healing as emotional support from others.

In his 1954 book, *Motivation and Personality*, psychologist Abraham Maslow identified a strong need for solitude as one of the characteristics of the 'self-actualized' individuals he studied. Maslow reported that nearly all of the 'psychologically healthy' people he researched said that they 'positively like solitude and privacy to a definitely greater degree than the average person'.[5] And encouragingly, there is an increasing body of research around not only the benefits of solitude, but also that a high preference for solitude might actually be associated with some positive personality traits. A 2023 study looked at whether people benefitted from a balance between hours spent in solitude and hours spent in social time. The results showed that although there was no such thing as the 'right' number of hours to spend in solitude, spending more hours alone was linked with reduced stress, as well as a feeling of freedom to choose and be oneself. Professor Netta Weinstein, the lead author of the study, said that 'the enforced lockdowns of the pandemic highlighted many of the long-lasting impacts that can occur when we are starved of interaction with other people. Yet this study highlights [that] time alone can leave us feeling less stress and free to be ourselves'.[6] As someone who requires a significant amount of alone time, the results of this study come as no surprise to me.

In Netta Weinstein, Heather Hansen and Thuy-vy Nguyen's 2024 book, *Solitude: The Science and Power of Being Alone*, the authors showcase the multitude of benefits that solitude can provide. They share findings from their collective, and rigorous, research gathered in numerous studies – including how solitude can provide time for calm and reflection, how it can help with emotional regulation, as well as how it can enhance our mood and psychological well-being.[7] Also, a 2023 research article by Weinstein for the University of Reading shared the results of 60 qualitative interviews that looked at the impacts of personality and mindset in relation to experiencing solitude as a positive thing. The study showed, among other things, that the qualities of curiosity and optimism were useful mindset tools for positive solitude; Weinstein concluded that by gaining an understanding of the mindset and personality traits of people who thrive in their alone time, 'we may be able to begin to mold solitude into a more welcoming and desirable space.'[8]

So with this in mind, let's find out from some of the single women I spoke to what their relationship to solitude actually looks like. Do they love it? Hate it? Or are they somewhere in the middle? I'm curious to know whether other single women revel in the alone time that they're afforded as a by-product of being single and childfree.

The Joy of Me Time

Of the various themes that came out of my conversations around solitude, it was the 'joy' of it that struck me the most. Almost all of the women I spoke to expressed a love of their time in solitude, telling me why they love it and how they spend it, from reading to working to just *being*. I'll start with a quote within a quote, from Susan (67, Toronto, Canada). She speaks of the fiercely independent actress, the late Katharine Hepburn:

> ❝ The actress Katharine Hepburn did a one and only interview with Dick Cavett, and she said something that I always quote (but not in relation to alcohol): 'Cold sober, I find myself absolutely fascinating.' And it's my favourite quote. It's like, I don't need anybody else. ❞

THRIVE SOLO

Perhaps we don't all find ourselves to be fascinating, but Katharine Hepburn's words speak very much to the idea that people *can* be content in their own company; and more than that, some people love their own company.

This view is backed up by Karen (51, London), who told me:

❝ My time alone takes a lot of beating. And I don't mean that to sound arrogant. It's not that I think I'm anything special, but I really do love spending a significant amount of my time in my own company.

Alone time is where I get to pursue the things that I love doing, like creating art, or reading a book for three hours, or spending time on self-care, like yoga or meditation, or walking in among the trees in the park near where I live.

In some ways I find more joy in the time I spend by myself than I do when I'm with other people. And that isn't to say I don't enjoy spending time with the people I love, because I do. It's just that I'm always happy to leave because I need a certain amount of time by myself for my own well-being. Ultimately, I'm happiest in solitude. ❞

Ileana (38, Northern California) told me that: 'The longer I'm single, the more I appreciate and really relish that time on my own.' She explained how she, too, likes to prioritise her solitude, saying that she recently told a good friend that she couldn't reschedule their meet-up because she was looking forward to spending time by herself, and she wasn't willing to give that up. Maddie (50, Bristol) tells me that she needs plenty of solo time in order to go out into the world. As she's got older, she's stopped seeing her need for alone time as a flaw. Maddie has realised that the time she requires to 'just sit and be', whether that's listening to a podcast or pottering around

Solitude

at home, is vital for her to be able to go out into the world and do what she needs to do.

Jess (42, London) told me that solitude 'gives you time to breathe because you can just sit, or have a bath, or just sit on the couch and be at peace with yourself. [. . .] Again, it's joy.' Jess added that solitude 'is a funny word because, for me, when you hear the word solitude, it kind of feels sad. It's a sad word. Like spinsterhood's a sad word, right? But it's not. To me solitude is peace and quiet.' Oh, I hear you, ladies! 'Sad' isn't a word I would ever use to describe my time alone.

What all these kinds of pursuits have in common is a feeling of connectedness. And it is through solitude that we can find that most profound fullness and connection . . . to *ourselves*. Ileana (38, Northern California) expresses this point so beautifully:

> ❛❛ I feel like with solitude, I understand it as a communion I have with myself and the world; I feel it's not lonely at all. I feel very connected, actually, and very at home in solitude. For me it's really vital. And if I'm missing that, or I don't have it, that's when I'll feel lonely. When I've got too much on my schedule, I'll start to feel a distance growing between me and myself, basically – solitude is the moment when that gap is bridged and we're able to reconnect again. ❜❜

Lara (51, Reading) is another who finds connection in solitude and for whom alone time is an overwhelmingly positive thing:

> ❛❛ I spend a lot of time going for walks on my own; I love walking in woods, so I do that pretty much every day because I just need that space to be part of the world, I guess, connected. And I've needed to be on my own for a very long time. Just a couple of days ago,

I had a short but intense row with my mother because potentially my uncle was going to take us away for my aunt's birthday. We were going to share a room, and I said I would like to offer to pay some money so I could have my own room. And my mum was like, what's wrong with you? But I need that space. I need to be on my own. **"**

All that is to say that solitude doesn't seem so bad after all, does it?

Being Lonely in Old Age

An assumption often made about single women who spend a significant amount of time alone is that they must be lonely, *and* that their loneliness will inevitably worsen as they get older. This is surely one of the most pervasive, irritating and borderline offensive assumptions made about singles – and one that most of us single ladies will have been met with at some point or another. *Who's going to look after you when you can no longer look after yourself?* While this isn't something I concern myself with, I'm aware that there are singles out there who do. However, it's worth pointing out that even if you're married with children, that is no guarantee that you *won't* be lonely in old age, or that you *will* have someone to look after you, if and when you can no longer look after yourself.

The reality is that it's anyone's guess whether your partner will still be around in 30 years. People die; people divorce; and people do not automatically build their parents a luxury granny annexe in a convenient spare wing of their home. Even if little Billy (aged seven) promised Mummy he would look after her when she gets old, big Billy may well have buggered off to Australia with his hot second wife by that point, only to be seen once every three years, if Mummy's lucky.

Solitude

Here's what Karen (51, London) had to say on this subject:

❝ I always think it's strange when people ask me if I worry about being lonely in my old age, just because I'm single. Loneliness isn't something that I feel often, if ever, and it certainly isn't an inevitability of being single. And when it comes to my later years – whether or not I'll be lonely, and what will happen if I can't look after myself – these aren't things I spend time thinking about because I choose to live my life in the here and now rather than worrying about what may or may not happen 20 years in the future. ❞

As Karen so rightly points out, being alone is not the same as being lonely. It's true that one can be alone *and* be lonely, but this is not the default setting. And for those single women who do feel lonely, perhaps if people stopped asking us about loneliness on a regular basis, we may not second-guess whether perhaps we *are* lonely, even if we're perfectly happy more often than not. Returning to Sara Maitland's book, *How to Be Alone*, she says:

❝ If you tell people enough times that they are unhappy, incomplete, possibly insane, and definitely selfish, there is bound to come a grey morning when they wake up with the beginnings of a nasty cold and wonder if they are lonely rather than simply 'alone'.[9] ❞

An interesting, and most definitely surprising, study was done in 2019 by Ashley E. Ermer and Christine M. Proulx, which looked at the association between social connectedness and emotional well-being among adults aged 62 and over. The results found that older people who felt most closely connected with other people were the ones who didn't have a partner; and that those who were either married or living with a partner did

THRIVE SOLO

not feel the same sense of 'social connectedness'.[10] In other words, the older single people were actually doing better in terms of loneliness than the older married or coupled people. Who'd have thunk it?

For me, never was my absence of loneliness (or my love of solitude) more apparent than during my time spent living alone in my small studio flat during the first Covid-19 lockdown. While there were concerns in the media about the 'poor single people' – and I mean no disrespect to those who loathed it and were terribly lonely, not to mention those who truly suffered – but, not to put too fine a point on it: I bloody loved it. Glorious, endless days of not having to socialise; 'not being able' to leave my beloved corner of South West London; long walks by the river every single day; neither the horror of home schooling, nor the dawning realisation that I no longer wanted to be with my partner; hours and hours spent turned inwards, engaged in the previously inconceivable luxury of 'working on myself'; and the first time in my entire adulthood when I was able to take a breath and work out what I actually wanted from my life. Not once did I get bored. Why would I when there is so much to learn? Here I was presented with the perfect opportunity to lean into the things I'd never had the time for before. It was a frickin' revelation.

And I wasn't the only one who actually enjoyed their solo time during the pandemic. Kerri (51, Brisbane) told me about her experience of the Covid-19 lockdowns, saying, 'Everyone was going nuts when we were having lockdowns back in Covid days, but it was barely a blip on my radar. My life during the pandemic barely changed. It was like this is what lockdown is, and this is what I'd normally do anyway.' Kaitlin (42, Nashville) told me about her thoughts on loneliness and her experience of the pandemic:

Solitude

❝ There's a big discrepancy between solitude and loneliness. I've experienced both. But the solitude aspect of it, you know, early in the pandemic – in Tennessee especially, it was never a shutdown, I was still going to work – I loved the fact that on the weekends I never felt pressured to go anywhere or do anything. I just got to come home, close the door and dive into whatever weird-ass thing I was into that day. I got really into history during the pandemic; I discovered this whole side of my personality that loves learning about history and major historical events. I just go from era to era, diving into some weird thing I've never thought of. Right now, I'm into Vikings! And I just love it – I love doing that. I listened to a 13-hour podcast on the origins of World War I very early on in the pandemic. The solitude didn't bother me for almost that whole year. ❞

And finally, Kim (61, St Petersburg, Florida) and Rachel (36, Scotland) both remind us that loneliness can also be present when surrounded by other people. Kim told me, 'I really don't feel lonely, and the time when I did feel lonely was when I was around my family or people who were trying to bring me down for being alone; trying to make me feel bad for being alone. But no, you can be lonely in a crowd.' And Rachel told a friend who'd asked her about loneliness that she's actually felt lonely when she's been in relationships. She also added that loneliness isn't necessarily the result of being single, but that it can be related to where you are in your own head – your mindset. I couldn't agree more with this. Poet and novelist May Sarton once said: 'Loneliness is the poverty of self; solitude is the richness of self.'[11] And it's my belief that loneliness is as much a state of mind as it is the result of one's circumstances – if not more so. With this attitude, there's no reason to be daunted with the prospect of alone time as we grow older.

THRIVE SOLO

Singlehood and Introversion

Interestingly, through my research, I started to notice a connection between women who are single and women who are introverted. Many of the single women I've spoken to have 'confessed' to being introverted. It may just be a coincidence – and I'm definitely not claiming to have done anything that qualifies as scientific research on the subject – but I can't help noticing this trait that seems to be present in a significant number of single women. And it goes without saying that not all single women are introverts, but I do wonder if those of us who are more comfortable with our single status also tend towards introversion, too?

Well, it turns out that there actually is evidence to back up my theory, and researchers have found that most singles are introverts rather than extroverts. A study that was published in the *Personality and Social Psychology Bulletin* revealed how certain personality traits predict who is more likely to be single, or in a relationship. Elaine Hoan, the lead author in the study, said that as marriage rates decline and more people live on their own, it transpires that single lives go beyond 'the misleading stereotype of the miserable single person'. Hoan went on to say that relationship status doesn't play 'as big of a role in one's overall life satisfaction as you may think' and that it's personality more than relationship status that determines who is happy and who isn't.[12]

What an Introvert Is . . . and Is Not

There is sometimes a misunderstanding around what actually constitutes either an introvert or an extrovert, my own personality traits being a good case in point. Because while introverts can be shy and quiet, I am neither of these. For example, the first time I told my mum that I was an introvert, she scoffed and

62

said something along the lines of 'Don't be ridiculous, you're about as far from an introvert as it gets.' And she's right in as much as I can be extremely sociable. But being an introvert does not *necessarily* mean that you're quiet or shy. And in my case, I have learned that my own personal brand of introversion is, actually, extroverted. Say what?!

Pip (39, Isle of Wight) and I talked about this during our interview, and her own experience very much echoes my own:

> ❝ I've realised what an introvert I am. I always thought I was an extrovert. Like when I'm with people, I'm literally the life and soul, I'm the loudest one; but my heart wants to be on this sofa, cuddled up on my own. I can't wait to get back from work each day, close that door. [. . .] Before, I felt like a bloody alien. I thought, what the hell is wrong with me? I'm like some sort of freak! Because inside I was fighting it – that's why I used to go out all the time. I used to say yes to everything, I was such a 'yes' person. And now I'm just like, no, I don't have to do that. I've accepted myself for it all now. That's huge. It's huge. ❞

Bella (70, Summerland, California), like both Pip and I, also enjoys being around other people and was initially unaware that she was an introvert:

> ❝ I actually wasn't sure what I was, and I did something I rarely do: take one of those scientifically validated tests of introversion. And I came across as clearly an introvert. But the reason I wasn't sure is because I do enjoy being around people. And I used to entertain a lot when I had a better house for entertaining (I'm in a small place now). So I just didn't know, but I am clearly an introvert. ❞

THRIVE SOLO

In actual fact, one of the main traits of being introverted – and the one that I identify with the very most – is that unlike extroverts, who require external stimulation to generate their energy, introverts need to be alone in order to recharge their batteries. So whereas an extrovert will seek out other people if their internal battery is running low, an introvert will do the exact opposite. Bella also relates to this aspect of introversion:

> ❝ I think I've become more introverted with age. But even [when I was] younger, I remember I would go to these conferences that would go on over the course of, say, three days, and they'd be intensely social. And when I got home and I'd stop in the office to pick up my mail, I just really did not want to see anyone. I didn't even want to say hi to anyone. ❞

Kristi (38, Estherville, Iowa) also relates strongly to the need to recharge through time spent alone, saying, 'I'm a bit of an introvert to begin with, and if I'm in a large group, and I've spent a large amount of time in a large group, I need to have me time just to recharge. I'm like, "Don't call me, don't talk to me!" I need to recentre myself and just get back to me before I give anybody else any energy.'

A 2003 article by Jonathan Rauch called 'Caring for Your Introvert' resonated with me more than a little bit. Rauch asks whether you know someone who needs hours of alone time every day; someone who can give an amazing presentation to a large audience, but who hates small talk; someone who has to be dragged to parties; or someone who rolls their eyes 'when accosted with pleasantries by people who are just trying to be nice'.[13] And therein lies the problem for us introverts – the lack of understanding about this personality type among extroverts (who, let's face it, are a majority) and cannot conceive why we would ever want to be alone, and who also tend to take offence at our need to remove ourselves from . . . them. At the age of

48, I still struggle with other people's perceptions of what my 'anti-socialness' means *to* them and *about* them. But the simple truth is that it's not about them, as I'm sure the introverts among you will understand.

With all of the above in mind, it's not hard to see that being an introvert can lend itself very well to being both single and childfree.

Learning to Embrace Solitude

But what about the extroverts among us for whom enjoying solitude doesn't come easily? How can we learn to embrace it? Although I enjoy solitude now, looking back, I vividly remember times in my life when being alone was far more painful than it was joyous. Moments – particularly at weekends – when I felt completely lost, uncomfortable in my own skin, and a pervasive feeling of emptiness would take over me. At the time, I assumed that the gaping hole I felt inside myself could only be filled by another person. How wrong I was. So if this is you, what can you do?

Whatever society tells us about relationships, it's a universal truth that when it comes down to it, happiness really does come from within. We're all familiar with this idea, and it's one that many great thinkers, philosophers and artists have long spoken about, from Marcus Aurelius to Aristotle, Dale Carnegie to Agnes Repplier, Helen Keller to Albert Camus, and Jimi Hendrix to Oprah. But still, many of us choose to ignore it – perhaps because it's easier to buy into the narrative that tells us we'll find happiness in a romantic partner or a child – but we do so at our peril. Kristi, who's 38 and has been single her whole life, agrees wholeheartedly that 'there's only one person who can make you happy, and that's you. You don't need someone's validation. You don't need someone to be there to be happy and to live a fulfilled life.'

THRIVE SOLO

Learning to embrace being alone is something that will serve us well, not least because happiness *is* an inside job. And while there is a general tendency for society to favour company over solitude, surely it's crucial for us as human beings to be *able* to sit comfortably with ourselves? Shouldn't we aspire to be able to spend time alone? Being single can act as a catalyst, forcing us to master the skill of being alone, which, whether or not we remain single, cannot fail to serve us well throughout the rest of our lives.

No matter whether we're in a romantic relationship or not, we will live this life and leave this life the same way we arrived: alone. It was only through my own journey of personal development that I came to realise that the feeling of disconnection I had previously experienced when alone wasn't the result of being single; I was, in fact, disconnected from *myself*. I believe that this misunderstanding is the reason why so many people are afraid of being alone and subsequently fall into relationships that aren't necessarily right for them because they, too, are trying to fill this void. Thinking a relationship will be the missing piece of the puzzle, we often fail to look inside ourselves for what it is we believe we're missing.

Karen (51, London) spoke beautifully to this when she told me about her most recent relationship:

> ❝ I've been single now for 11 years, happily so, but before I got together with my most recent ex-boyfriend, it was a different story. I wasn't in a great place in my life and was desperately searching for someone to 'make me happy'. I was convinced that a relationship would be the missing piece of the puzzle and when I found it, I would feel complete. But the opposite happened.
>
> Not long after my ex and I had moved in together, I realised that the problem had never been the lack of relationship, it had been about me and the relationship

Solitude

I had with myself. When we split, I finally started doing the work on myself and my mindset, and it slowly dawned on me that happiness had eluded me not because I had been single, but because I had been disconnected from myself. I now wax lyrical to all of my friends about happiness coming from inside of us. I'm sure it drives them crazy, but it's so, so true! 🗨

If we continue to believe that our happiness needs to come from another person, then we will never feel at ease in our own company, let alone embrace solitude. But when we get to a place where we're able to cultivate feelings of happiness within ourselves, then we can also find the deep joy that solitude can bring. It's my belief that we should actually be far more concerned about those people who struggle to be on their own than those who appreciate and enjoy their alone time. As Jess (42, London) says: 'Solitude, I think, is something to be enjoyed – but not a lot of people can. [. . .] They are completely incapable of being on their own. And I find that quite sad. So I think in that respect, we're quite blessed.' What she said.

Jean (67, Clearwater, Florida) is another who has had to learn to embrace solitude, telling me: 'There's this very fine line between solitude and this feeling of isolation, so I've been playing around with that more, which then makes solitude even more delicious and precious.' She went on to say how she has learned to lean into solitude when being alone feels hard:

> 🗨 I remember being asked by a mentor, what are your lifesavers? What are those things that fill you up and bring you joy? Find those. Those things that fill you up. Notice where you're bright and shining. That's probably one thing about learning to be comfortable alone, like, can you sit with that? And if you sit with it and drop below it, not wallow in it, but get to the other

THRIVE SOLO

side of that, it's a whole different ball game. Learn to be at peace in the moment. Learn to be comfortable in that moment of solitude, because then you can be comfortable with another person. **JJ**

Jean's final point circles us back to the importance of being comfortable in our own company. Because unless we are comfortable within ourselves, we will not be comfortable in a relationship. Before we connect with another person, we must first connect with ourselves.

Final Thoughts

I have to say that it was such a pleasure to hear so many other women waxing lyrical about their love and appreciation of solitude. It wasn't so long ago that I still wondered what was wrong with me that I felt such a strong desire and need to be by myself a significant amount of the time. These days, I relish it more than ever because I've given myself permission to just go with it, rather than fight it. I no longer say yes to things when what I mean is no. I've come to learn that my solitude is precious to me, and I will no longer sacrifice it in order to look 'normal' to other people. It's who I am.

Speaking of other people, as you've already heard from Bella, Pip and Karen, loving solitude doesn't mean we don't love and adore the time we spend with our family and friends. Quite the opposite. I love that time more because I've given myself what I need first and can subsequently show up as my best self.

Although relationships are *one* of the cornerstones of a healthy and happy life, there is much value to be found in time spent alone and, for some, solitude is not just something we love; it is something we need and actively seek out. Solitude is necessary for our mental health and happiness, as well as giving us the time and space needed to pursue working on ourselves. Some might even say that it's one of the most significant advantages of a solo life.

—Podcast Pearls—

'I just need time to myself. I love it. It recharges me. It relaxes me. It makes me better able to be a good conversation or action partner when I am with other people. I think if I didn't get enough time alone, that would be a problem.'

— Bella (70, Summerland, California)

4

CAREERS AND FINANCIAL INDEPENDENCE

'Had I got married and had children, I simply wouldn't have been able to maintain the hours or the effort that I put into my career. And that, for me, is what makes me feel good.'

— DRISHTI (33, MUMBAI)

You can't have it all. Nobody can. When you have a partner and kids, your energy and focus are divided in a way that they're not when you're single and childless. It's not a judgement, it's just a fact of life that is never more apparent than when it comes to careers. It goes without saying that there are, of course, plenty of mums out there doing amazing work in amazing careers, but the pull of family life is unavoidable – especially when small children are involved. For women with partners and kids, the potential impact of this set-up on their careers can be profoundly negative, and by the same token the impact of *not* having a partner and kids can be profoundly positive. Because one thing those of us who are single and without kids don't have is the constant push–pull of daily family obligations balanced with the pressures of work – and the struggle is real. I've seen it in the lives of my own friends and family members.

THRIVE SOLO

While juggling family responsibilities, it simply isn't possible to be as laser-focused on a career as it is when you're free of those obligations. In a 2022 UK survey of 2,264 working mothers, 68 per cent stated that their careers had 'stalled' as a direct result of having children.[1] Similarly, the Fawcett Society has estimated that almost a quarter of a million working mothers in the UK have left their jobs. Digging deeper, it found that one in 10 mums quit their jobs due to childcare pressures and two-fifths of working mums have turned down a promotion due to childcare pressures. This isn't surprising when considering it was also found that only 31 per cent of working mothers have access to the flexible working arrangements necessary to juggle their family lives, and 85 per cent of them struggle to find jobs that will allow for their childcare needs.[2] Quite frankly, my heart goes out to working mums and I most certainly do not envy them.

In early 2024, *The Economist* published an article entitled 'How Motherhood Hurts Careers'. It stated that, worldwide, 95 per cent of men aged 25 to 54 are in the workforce, whereas for women in the same age category, the figure is only 52 per cent. The article also shared the results of a study by Princeton University and the London School of Economics that found that what is described as the 'motherhood penalty' means that almost 25 per cent of women leave the labour force in the first year after having children; after a further five years, 17 per cent of them are still absent, and 15 per cent are still absent after 10 years.[3] Again . . . harsh.

The above numbers confirm that having a family undeniably makes it harder for women to reach a certain level of success in working life. It just is what it is. In order to get to the top of any field, what's required is a combination of absolute focus, minimal distraction and a sort of single-minded determination, coupled with the necessary amount of time and capacity.

For my own part, I have no doubt that I would not be doing what I'm doing now had I got married and had children. At this point in my life – producing, hosting and editing a podcast, co-hosting a second, new podcast (*Three Single Women*), running a growing membership, writing – I work evenings and weekends in addition to full-time hours, and have been doing so for the last two and a half years. I'm not saying this is necessarily a good thing, or something I'll be able to (or should) keep up forever, but the point is that I'm free to throw absolutely everything I have at these endeavours because I want to. I have the luxury of uninterrupted time and space to focus, almost exclusively, on this work. And I see this as a *good* – and perhaps underrated – thing. Let's explore this more. . .

We Get a Lot out of Work

We've all heard the term 'career woman' and its (often negative) connotations: the ruthless female, not a maternal bone in her body, pursuing success at the expense of all else. The implication tends to be that a woman driven by her work is somehow *not* a good thing. But this negative narrative undermines the fact that for many women, their careers provide a huge amount of fulfilment and meaning. To put it simply: we can get a lot out of it.

And this career drive is not necessarily motivated by some underlying desire either to *avoid* having children or as a way of masking a desire *to* have them. Nor is it always that we're running away from relationships or that we're scared of intimacy. Despite what the bad press will have you believe, sometimes a woman's work is just fabulous in and of itself. Sometimes a woman's career can be as all-consuming, significant and purposeful as the work of being a mum. And sometimes ending up not having children can be a happy twist of fate that enables

THRIVE SOLO

you to throw yourself fully into the thing you were put here to do. So conditioned are we by the traditional expectation of marriage and babies that we sometimes forget there are plenty of other things in life that can bring us just as much joy, and work can be one of them!

Kate (55, London), who has written two books – *Losing It: How We Popped Our Cherry Over the Last 80 Years* and *The First Time: True Tales of Virginity Lost & Found*[4] – speaks to this well. She told me that she's not sure she would have found the time to write her books had she committed to family life, and not writing her books would have been a sad thing for her. Kate went on to explain:

> It's a bit of a cliché, but following my joy, following my passions in my creative life, has been one of my greatest loves. Writing a book is a little bit like birth. It's something that literally comes from inside you – you create it, limb by limb. It's unique. It wouldn't exist unless you did, and after you die, it will still be there. We all contribute to the world in different ways, and that [Kate's books] is one of mine. I love having the freedom to do stuff like that, and I'm not sure I would have if I'd had a family. There's a limit to the places and spaces in which I can point my focus, and I'm so grateful that I get to live a creative life of writing.

Drishti (33, Mumbai) has an extremely demanding career in computer science, which she loves. Her family were shocked when she left her home town – and them – for her work, and were concerned that she'd be alone forever if she carried on putting so much into her work. But Drishti explains:

> My work brings me joy. Yes, I work incredibly hard, but I also find it rewarding and challenging in all the best ways, and it fulfils me. Had I got married and had

Careers and Financial Independence

children, I simply wouldn't have been able to maintain the hours or the effort that I put into my career. And that, for me, is what makes me feel good. 〃

Rachel (36, Scotland) is also someone who certainly gets a lot out of her work. She explained that she is 'a bit of a butterfly' who has always wanted 'to experience all sorts of different things in terms of careers, and I really get a huge amount out of that'. Being single and not having children has allowed her to experiment, switch things up, lean into her work and 'do something that makes me feel something, you know, and that's always been really important to me'. More to come on Rachel's different jobs shortly.

Lindsey (45, West Sussex) feels that it's a been a privilege to be able to pour all her energy just into her career. She specialises in working with children and babies who are born with cerebral palsy, which has made her aware of the huge impact that having a child with additional needs can have on parenting and family life in general. And it's not just parents of children with additional needs who struggle, it's her colleagues, too. Lindsey says:

❝ I work predominantly with women in my profession, and they're constantly having to change appointments or move things around because they can't do something, or they've got a child to pick up. I can see that they're just juggling it all. Whereas I can just focus on my career, and have the energy for it. I'm not juggling things. I get overwhelmed very easily when there's a lot going on, so I think that the load of juggling a career that I'm really passionate about and having a child is something I really would've struggled with. 〃

In addition, Lindsey has been able to do charity work with children, which she may well not have had the time for if she'd had her own children.

75

Similarly, Kailee (30, Jacksonville, North Carolina), who is in the process of starting her own business, feels fortunate to be 'able to do things like pursue continuing education, which gives me more skills and knowledge for practice in my field'. Kailee also really appreciates having 'the unstructured time when I get home; just having that energy, feeling like I really get to recharge my batteries. I'm not on overdrive, hopping from my job right into making dinner, and other things that are involved with families.' She adds, 'For me, having that time to devote to my career – that's what gives me a sense of meaning and purpose, and such a sense of balance. So I feel really fortunate that I have that.'

When I asked Kailee if she thought she'd be starting a business if she'd had a family, she replied, 'Absolutely not. If I had to balance that with a family and a second job, I'd be overwhelmed. I probably wouldn't be the upbeat, happy person I am most days!'

Circling back to my original point, interestingly, none of the women I talked to about this topic struck me as fitting the ruthless and hard-nosed stereotype of a 'career woman'. Instead, they are simply women with the time and space to pursue their career as much as they wish, and for many this is clearly an appealing prospect.

Career Flexibility

As we touched on in Chapter 1, being single and childfree allows us to have more flexibility specifically when it comes to our careers, too. Let's dig deeper now and see how this can play out in different ways.

Careers and Financial Independence

Flexibility to Try Different Jobs

When you do not have the responsibility of a family to consider, there is an ability to try out new and different things when it comes to work (based on your own personal circumstances, of course). There's something so wonderful about having the freedom to try something that might be a complete departure from what you were previously doing, without having to worry about the impact it might have on somebody else – or indeed without having to deal with any opinions or judgements. You have complete autonomy to design a working life that suits you.

Rachel (36, Scotland) is someone who has always enjoyed being able to concentrate on her career and is very positive about the impact that not having either a partner or a child has had on her work life. In particular, she appreciates that she has been able to decide what work suits her best at different points in her life; she's had the freedom to explore various options. Rachel started her career as a dancer, but when nothing came of this, she followed the 'natural next thing' for her, which was a career in biology. This change eventually led Rachel into nature conservation – working for a small charity on their peatland restoration – which is where she still works now. Rachel loves her job. She enjoys being outside in the natural environment and that's where she now spends much of her time. However, the flexibility of Rachel's life has also allowed her to cut down to four days a week and take on another job, supporting a girl with multiple sclerosis, which she finds incredibly fulfilling. In Rachel's words, 'being single and not having kids has allowed me the freedom to chop and change', and this has allowed her to keep her career varied and interesting.

Sue's (60, London) childfree status has allowed her to be flexible during her career in arts PR. Sue told me that not having children has enabled her to work part-time as a freelancer, meaning she has the freedom to take on a range of varied and interesting projects that appeal to her, while enjoying the lifestyle she always wanted, i.e. working part-time rather than full-time. This is possible because she doesn't have the overheads that come with children and isn't obliged to work more, or in a better-paid area that might not interest her as much, such as retail PR or consumer PR. She is free to work in the area she enjoys and for the amount of time she wants to in order to sustain a solo life.

When I reflect on my own career, I can also relate to enjoying the freedom to try new and varied things. For example – as mentioned in the introduction – I have (among other things) been a radio producer, a PA, a cleaner, a detective, a coach, a barista, a podcaster, a creator of a membership community . . . and now a writer! Not having to worry about a partner and/or children has meant I've been able to enjoy a working life that has taken many twists and turns, and I've been fortunate enough to be able to focus on what I truly want to do in my career. I've never felt tied to a 'stable' job that my heart isn't in or motivated by those aspects of a job that I might have prioritised had I had the responsibility of a family. Like Rachel and Sue, I feel lucky and privileged to enjoy a varied career.

I would like to add here that, yes, there is an argument to say that if you have a partner who has a steady income, then you may be able to try out new things, work in a different way, and have the freedom to enjoy a varied career too; but for the purposes of this book, my point is that being both single and childfree means you have a freedom that is not necessarily available to you when you have a family of your own.

Flexibility to Work Where You Want

Another aspect of flexibility that single women can enjoy is the relative ease with which we can up sticks and move for our work, without having to consider anyone else.

Careers and Financial Independence

Annie (44, San Antonio, Texas), for example, was able to move from Kentucky to California to Austin, and reflects that this was made easier – or even possible – by the fact that she didn't have a partner. For Annie, this all comes back to having the freedom to make these decisions herself.

Likewise, Kaitlin (42, Nashville) most likely wouldn't be living in Nashville had she ended up getting married and starting a family. Kaitlin works in the wine business and a few years ago, she was able to move spontaneously from South Carolina to Oregon for her job. She is happy that she has been able to seize opportunities due to her ability to 'do things quickly'.

Sometimes moving for a job is motivated by necessity rather than purely following opportunity or adventure. Drea (38, North East England) was able to move during the 2008 recession to find work elsewhere, having been made redundant. She told me that there were no suitable jobs where she lived that provided both her required salary and the challenge she was looking for in her work, so she had to move. Her newly single status made this easier, as she explained:

> ❝ I had just broken up with my boyfriend at the time. On reflection, if I'd still been with that person I wouldn't have moved. And if I hadn't moved, I wouldn't have gone through the different things I've done, and grown this really amazing, wonderful, challenging and enlightening career that I absolutely love, and that I'm super passionate about. I wouldn't have been able to do any of that; I would have compromised [by taking] a job in my local area instead.
>
> Today, I also wouldn't be able to travel for work at the drop of a hat like I do. I can do these things because I don't have to think about anyone else. I've worked so hard in my career to be able to do this – and to do what I want to do – [for which] I'm super grateful. ❞

THRIVE SOLO

Ultimately, not having a partner or children means you are able to move quickly and easily for your career, should the opportunity arise. You don't need to consider your partner's work or your children's schools. Instead, you are able to confidently take the bull by the horns, if the opportunity is right for you, instead of having to mull over a once-in-a-lifetime chance because you need to consider its impact on your family.

Take me, for example. Once I had agreed to write this book, I realised that something was going to have to give if I was going to be able to write it while also keeping both my podcast and my membership community going. So I quit the job I had in a coffee shop, rented out my flat in London for a year, and moved back to Dorset – all within a very short space of time. It was very much thanks to my single, childfree status that I was able to make those decisions so quickly. And, I might add, it was being single and childfree that made me *willing* to take such relatively extreme measures in order to further my career.

Flexibility to Take Risks

We all have a very different tolerance level when it comes to taking risks, but in matters of career and finances, it's fair to say that being responsible only for oneself means we're more likely – and often able – to take a leap into the unknown. This is because if we take a risk and it all goes pear-shaped, well, we only have ourselves to blame and worry about. But take a risk when there are three small mouths to feed, and much more is at stake.

As someone who is quite prone to taking risks, I'm grateful that there is no one else depending on me when I invariably decide to do something 'risky'. When I left the career I'd worked so hard for at Radio 2, for example, to become a detective, I did so because I knew that for me there was more to life, and I had to try something else. But taking the plunge to leave my comfort

Careers and Financial Independence

zone and become a detective also turned out to be the wrong path for me, so I took a risk again. This time I handed in my notice, once more leaving a safe and secure job that came with a pension and healthcare, with the intention of following my heart and changing my life for the better. I became a part-time barista in a coffee shop and also worked as my sister's cleaner so that I could fund my new podcast. This is the move that has ultimately led to my work today. The chances I would have done all of the above had I been married and had children? Slim to none.

Other women I spoke to feel the same way as I do regarding our freedom to take risks. One is Julie (43, Walla Walla, Washington), a third-generation dentist:

    ❝ I have this drive to be very untraditional in my career and to push myself. Being single and childfree takes a lot of pressure off me, I think, in the sense that I can cut my income, I can cut my days, or I can really pivot in a lot of ways because it doesn't affect anybody else. I always say, 'Hey, if I have to eat beans and rice for a few months, who cares?' It doesn't matter. I don't have to pay for kids' education, or clothes, or sports, or family holidays. This lack of obligation takes a big burden off me; it allows me to experiment, to take some risks; to chase some dreams that may or may not go anywhere. In the last couple of years, I've been really pushing towards less clinical work and more creative work, and nobody's losing their quality of life because I'm not in the office producing a large income. ❞

And Bella (70, Summerland, California) was able to take a risk when she decided to move from the East Coast to the West Coast. We heard in Chapter 1 how Bella took a one-year sabbatical from her job at the University of Virginia and went to work at the University of California, Santa Barbara. When

THRIVE SOLO

her sabbatical came to an end, Bella realised that she wanted to stay because she'd fallen in love with the place. She told me that because she didn't have a spouse or children, she was able to take the big financial risk of giving up her job and a tenured academic position. But risk it she did, and with a positive outcome. Bella is now an academic affiliate in the Department of Psychological & Brain Sciences at the University of California, Santa Barbara, and is very happily living her solo life on the West Coast of the US.

Financial Independence

Of course, hand in hand with the topic of careers comes finance. Let's face it, all but the most financially fortunate among us can relate to the struggles and often unfair disadvantages that come as a by-product of being single. In the UK, the 'discount' in council tax for single people is roughly 25 per cent, rather than the 50 per cent it should be as a solo person rather than a couple. And don't even get me started on the single supplements that mean we have to pay *extra* money for using *fewer* resources – seriously, wtf?! From 'couple discounts', to receiving free healthcare via your partner's health insurance, to splitting household bills and food costs, the list of injustices is seemingly endless.

While there may be downsides when it comes to finances and being single, let's not forget what the alternative could look like. Studies show that financial challenges are one of the leading causes of marriage and relationship break-ups. A 2018 UK study carried out by family law specialists Slater and Gordon found that money worries are at the top of the list of reasons why couples break up, with one in five people saying money was the biggest cause of marital strife.[5] And a poll conducted by DivorceMagazine.com also found financial issues to be the leading cause of divorce. Dan Couvrette, the publisher of the magazine, said that 'During the divorce, the two most contentious issues are usually finances and children – in that order.'[6] Hmmm . . . interesting.

But when it comes to us single ladies, is there *anything* for us to celebrate in matters of money? Well, I'm going to go out on a limb and say that, yes, there is. There is an empowering freedom and independence that comes alongside having full control over our financial lives. The mere fact that we can spend our money on exactly what we like, however much or little it may be (and trust me, I'm more au fait with the latter), is something worth celebrating. Financial independence, whatever that looks like for you, *is* a big deal and we should celebrate it.

When we are feeling flush, we can splurge guilt-free on a pair of £300 jeans and get our eyebrows done every month, splash out on a solo trip to Nepal and fritter our hard-earned cash on as much pointless crap as we like. Alternatively, if money is in short supply, we can eat tinned soup for supper every night for a month without being judged or moaned at. We are also spared the pitfalls and irritations of a joint account that our partner uses, yet again, to spend money on gaming/cycling/DIY equipment. More equipment?! Or how about you have your heart set on that cute little Airbnb for the bank holiday weekend, but your partner flat-out refuses to pay for it, telling you it's a waste of money because you'll have 'nothing to show for it'? Nothing to show for it?! Rude. Think of the photos! The memories! Joking aside, financial conflict in relationships is *real* for many people.

Freedom from Financial Conflict

Several of the women I spoke to had stories about financial conflict in some of their friends' relationships. Susan (67, Toronto) told me about friends of hers who discuss hiding certain purchases from their partner and keeping them a secret, or lying about the cost. To Susan, this seems like unnecessary stress in your life.

Susan also talked about a financial issue that comes up for her 23-year-old niece and her live-in boyfriend, who has a tendency to comment on the things she buys. For example, she might come home having bought three red peppers and be quizzed about why she bought three when they only need two. As Susan pointed out, who cares?! Susan's niece frequently regales her aunt with tales of being made to feel guilty for buying things that make her happy, which clearly isn't a healthy situation.

And Lisa Jansen (40, Auckland), an author we'll hear more from in the next chapter, told me that some friends of hers recently had a big argument because the husband wanted to use extra money they had for a new truck and the wife wanted to redo the kitchen. Lisa explained that in the end he 'won' because last year they did a big, fancy holiday that she wanted to do, so it was his 'turn'. Upon hearing this, Lisa felt relieved that she didn't have to make such compromises and can spend her money how she likes.

Gráinne (41, Ireland) also shared a story about a friend who was in a bad way financially, despite earning a good wage, because her husband is so irresponsible with money. Gráinne told me that this emphasised to her the importance of being able to control her own money. The stress is on her alone, and financially she's probably far behind her married counterparts, but overall she appreciates the freedom she has.

Christine (53, Atlanta, Georgia), too, has seen the trouble that finances can cause in a relationship, through the experiences of some of her friends, even to the point where couples are forced to stay together when they don't want to:

Careers and Financial Independence

❝ I know of quite a few couples who essentially stay married because they can't afford to live separately. I even know of one divorced couple who still live together in the same house – just on different floors – because they can't buy each other out of their share of the house. It makes me feel damn proud that I am paying my own way without anyone else's income (even if it'd be nice to have a back-up sometimes!).

I also knew of an older couple who both had serious health issues in their old age, and who both needed extra help at home, but there was only enough money to pay for one home assistant. Guess who got the bulk of the care? (The man, of course.) The woman later told me, in a quiet moment, that she had made a big mistake in not insisting on keeping her own money separate from her husband's when they first got married. Whenever I feel sad that I have no financial back-up, I think of this older lady, and I'm very grateful and proud of my financial independence. ❞

So, while us single ladies may experience challenges in certain areas of our financial lives, the conflict that can arise as a result of joint finances is something we needn't concern ourselves with.

Economic Empowerment

As single women, the independence that comes with managing our own finances can be empowering. Sinead (50, Dublin), for example, absolutely loves her financial independence. She told me that it motivates her to strive harder with her business because she knows she has to pay the bills. Here's what else Sinead shared with me:

85

THRIVE SOLO

❝ I can come and go as I please, and I can spend my money on experiences, however I like. I'm doing up my apartment at the moment and it's my budget. I'll spend it how I want and cut costs wherever I like too. I'm really lucky that I'm able to rent out a spare room so that I have an income from that.

I'm much happier being financially independent because I just feel that I don't have to apologise for spending my money, and I'm not under pressure to spend money too. Being financially independent gives me so much pride and makes me feel better about myself. ❞

In fact, I was pleasantly surprised by how strongly the women I spoke to felt about having total control of their finances, despite the struggles that many face. For example, Jess (42, London), told me:

❝ If I have a tough few months financially, which does happen, then I know I can rein in my spending until I'm back on track. But I love knowing that my money is mine. I make it; I spend it; I save it. And saving for a trip or that one thing you're working hard for, and being able to finally get it, is a great feeling ❞

Rebecca (46, St Albans) feels a similar way and says that she loves knowing that she's supporting herself financially through her own business and derives great satisfaction from it. And Lindsey (45, West Sussex) spoke of the gratitude she feels for being born in the UK in a time when women now have financial independence. She said: 'So many women don't have this, and this makes me feel sad. Financial autonomy enables freedom.' It's not something she takes for granted.

And finally, Kriss (53, Portland, Oregon) told me how she feels totally 'badass' about her financial independence, particularly having grown up in a 'patriarchal family' as the only

Careers and Financial Independence

daughter. Kriss explains she was never 'expected or encouraged to figure this [money] shit out . . . and I did!' She now takes pride in the fact that she has managed to carve out a life financed all on her own. She explains:

    ᶜᶜ I own my home; I pay for my things; I explore options; I save; I spend . . . all under my own direction and I'm doing really well with it! Being independent has led me to learn how to fix shit in my house (I replaced an electrical outlet and installed a dimmer switch on my living room lighting); learn about financial planning and investing (I will retire early, dammit); learn how to start my own business; save for travel, or shoes, or remodelling, or whatever the fuck I want. It has led to me growing, and that is priceless! **ᴶᴶ**

So, whatever the state of our own finances, let's keep reminding ourselves of the fact that being 100 per cent in control of our money can be hugely empowering and, as Kriss says, it can also be an opportunity to learn and grow. However challenging our finances can be as single women, being forced to learn and grow is always a win.

Final Thoughts

We've heard from many women in this chapter regarding both careers and money. So, what have we learned?

First, when it comes to the working lives of single women, there is no doubt that, in many ways, we're afforded the freedom to focus on and embrace our careers in a way that is significantly harder for those who are married or partnered with children. And it's not necessarily the case that single working women are ambitious and driven to the exclusion of all else; it's simply that not having a family of our own means we're more able to

THRIVE SOLO

throw ourselves with abandon into whatever job or pursuit we may be engaged in. We all know that having a family can be incredibly fulfilling, meaningful and joyful, but so can a career that we love and that works for us.

And as for our finances? Well, as I just mentioned, there's no getting away from the fact that being a woman on our own can be challenging when it comes to money. But there is also an empowering freedom and independence that comes alongside having full control over our financial lives. We're not beholden to the restrictions that a partner can impose on how we choose to spend our money, nor are we at risk of getting into financial hardship or conflict due to the actions of anyone other than ourselves. There is so much power in that.

—Podcast Pearls—

'My career was this thing that I kept coming back to. It's tied up in autonomy and freedom. Part of being an aspiring artist was, for me, always tied up with being single and not having kids – the freedom it affords you is something that is underrated. It allowed me to focus on pursuing my dream of writing.'

— Gina (55, Los Angeles)

5

SOLO TRAVEL

*'With all of the noise gone, I could really
hear what was going on inside.'*

— LAURA (54, MELBOURNE)

There is no doubt that travelling solo (I'm talking for pleasure, not work, here) is something that some people wouldn't even conceive of doing. And in my experience, telling someone that you're going on a solo trip tends to elicit any (or all) of the following questions:

- Don't you get scared travelling on your own?
- That's very brave of you; I wish I had the guts to do that!
- What if you get unwanted attention?
- What about eating in restaurants alone?
- Don't you get lonely not having anyone to talk to?
- What's the point of seeing a beautiful sunset on the beach by yourself; it's not really the same, is it?

The last time I checked, a beautiful sunset looked equally beautiful whether I was looking at it by myself or with someone else, because, funnily enough, the beauty of nature doesn't

THRIVE SOLO

alter depending on who you're with. As for not having anyone to talk to, I've always found that I talk to *far more* people when I'm on holiday by myself (more on this later). Eating in restaurants alone? Nobody cares. And when it comes to the so-called scary stuff, foreign countries don't suddenly morph back to caveman times at the mention of the words 'female traveller' (sabre-toothed tigers are not roaming the streets in search of lone, female prey). OK, I'm being facetious, but is taking a solo holiday as lonely, dangerous and unfulfilling as some people perceive it to be?

Well, not according to the stats, because the research shows that solo travel has been trending upwards since 2016, and that women in particular, in many parts of the world, are showing an increased interest in travelling alone. The data shows that 85 per cent of solo travellers are women, 72 per cent of women in the US have taken a solo trip, and 54 per cent of British females are more likely to travel alone than they were just a few years ago. And interestingly, in 2022, the greatest increase in solo travellers was in women over the age of 65.[1]

Enjoying solo travel doesn't always come naturally and can be a challenge financially, but it can also be a journey (pun intended) in and of itself. As Rachel (36, Scotland) knows from her solo travels in the UK, there can be both ups and downs to holidaying alone, just as there can when travelling with someone else. She talked to me about eating out alone and how 'sometimes you have these lonely dinners on your own, which sometimes can be a nice thing because you can just sit with a book and read while you're eating. But other times you can think about how nice it would be to sit with somebody else and have a chat.'

Kate (55, London), who now loves to travel solo, told me it took her time to get to the point of enjoying travel by herself too. She explained:

Solo Travel

ff I think on the journey to becoming a good solo traveller, there are hiccups along the way, 100 per cent. When I think back to some of my early trips, they were quite discombobulating at times, especially before the internet. So when there was no way to connect on WhatsApp or Instagram – that's when I was really by myself. It took me a while to find my travel legs. JJ

Maddie (50, Bristol) is another woman who wasn't initially convinced by travelling alone, explaining that 'taking a solo holiday was frightening, but something I knew I needed to do for myself to prove that I could, otherwise I felt I was keeping myself in some sort of cage.' So she bit the bullet and took a trip to Martha's Vineyard in the US, despite her discomfort: 'I wouldn't say that I felt entirely comfortable. There was still a part of me that was like, "Oh, I feel a bit weird that I'm on my own. Maybe people are looking at me!" And I didn't always feel comfortable eating out in the evening.' Despite her initial reservations, she said that 'I was just so proud of myself for doing it. And I didn't shy away from doing any of the things I really wanted to do – I did them all! It was brilliant. And I proved to myself, well yeah, I can do it, and it's cool!'

Undoubtedly, there are considerations that need to be taken into account when planning a solo trip, not least of which is the expense. Not only can you not split the cost of a room or hiring a car with someone, but there is also often a single supplement that is added when you book a room for one person. Safety is another factor (though this is true for every traveller), and women can be seen as an easy target. As well as using common sense and taking the same precautions as you would anywhere, it's a good idea to research your intended destination in advance to see if there are specific concerns, and to read up on tips from women who have already travelled solo there.

THRIVE SOLO

For my own part, solo travel has allowed me to step out of my comfort zone and build on my internal sense of resilience and confidence (more on this to come). For others, the thought of taking off to the other side of the world by yourself might currently scare the living daylights out of you. If this is you, read on: you just might find enough inspiration in the next few pages to change your mind.

Connecting with Other People

One of the main benefits of travelling solo that I hear time and time again is how, ironically, you tend to meet and connect with far more people than you would as part of a couple. (Of course this depends on your personality type – not everyone is able to or wants to talk to strangers, and that's fine, too.)

As Rachel (36, Scotland) told me: 'You kind of stay in your little insular group if you're travelling with someone else. But when I have been away on my own, I definitely find I make the effort to speak to other people, or people will more actively approach you.'

Maddie backed up this view when she told me about her aforementioned solo holiday:

❝ I remember eating out at this little pizza place and the staff were so sweet because I was there eating alone. This guy came out from the kitchen and gave me a local newspaper. And another guy came in and was playing the piano and asked me, 'Are you OK for me to play the piano?' And the staff came out from the kitchen and chatted to me, and I thought to myself, 'This is really lovely!' Now, this would not have happened if I'd been with somebody else – because I wouldn't have been outward focused; I would have been insular while I was with that other person. ❞

Solo Travel

This is something I resonate deeply with as it was very much my own experience when I took a solo road trip in the US back in October 2011. When the time came to collect my hire car from a multi-storey car park located by Boston's waterfront, the guy from the hire firm gave me the choice between a giant seven-seater Chrysler Town & Country and a far more suitable (but far less amusing and ironic) Toyota. So off I drove in the former, with some printed-out maps of my route to guide me. I had Indigo Girls blaring out of the speakers, and a giant smile on my face. I spent two weeks driving around New England: from Massachusetts to Maine, to New Hampshire to Vermont, back into Massachusetts to Connecticut, and ending up back in Boston.

While, of course, much of my time was spent alone in my car, several of my core memories from that trip involve unexpected but wonderful encounters with people who crossed my path completely by chance. These include a delightful dinner eating fresh lobster in Provincetown, Massachusetts, with two other female travellers I randomly met at my guest house, the Secret Garden Inn; an evening spent watching a band at the Bee's Knees Bar & Restaurant in Morrisville, Vermont, having met two of the band members the previous day; and a couple of hours spent sitting on a bench in the sunshine outside The Bookstore in Lenox, Massachusetts, chatting to the owner about life, love and James Taylor.

It's incredible how interactions with total strangers can not only fill your heart with joy, but also remind you of the incredible power of connection, albeit with people you will likely never meet again. I have no doubt that had I been travelling with somebody else, I would have missed out on all of those life-affirming experiences.

Author and modern-day nomad Lisa Jansen (40, Auckland) also talked about this when I interviewed her about her solo travels through New Zealand in a camper van over four and a half years:

THRIVE SOLO

❝ For me, what I've really appreciated about [travelling alone] is meeting other people. I think when you travel solo, you're more open to meeting other people. Especially for someone like me who has very limited people energy, I think if I were travelling with someone – whether a partner or a friend – that would be all the people energy I had, and all the interaction I would need, so I would be even less motivated to go and meet other people. But I've met so many amazing people on my solo travels during the last few years, and before. When you're on your own you just automatically put yourself out there more. And you probably also just look more approachable. So I really love that about solo travelling. ❞

Kate, who we heard from earlier, is a seasoned solo traveller, and has used travelling alone as an excuse to work on photographic projects that have enabled her to connect with a fabulous mixture of perfect strangers. When she's away on her travels, Kate takes her camera, literally meets people on the street, and takes photos of them. She told me that:

❝ It's something I've just naturally gravitated towards. Travelling in southern Italy, I see a lot of amazing older women who I suspect don't get noticed in the way that I feel they should. And so it felt quite natural to approach them. Often, we don't speak the same language, so this is all done by gesticulation! I started a series of portraits and it's just been so enjoyable. It's a great confidence-booster to have those conversations [and interactions] with people you don't know. And it's really nice to make something at the end that looks great, and to then be able to show them the image. ❞

Kate told me that she has loved her solo travels, and that her camera has allowed her to 'connect with people all the time. My camera has been my passport into other people's lives.'

Travel without Compromise

At the end of 2019, I travelled alone to Vis Island, off the coast of Croatia – a beautiful and unspoilt place that reminded me of Majorca or the Greek Islands, minus the over-development of your average Mediterranean enclave. I flew from London to Split, took a ferry from Split to Vis Town, and then a coach from Vis Town to the picture-perfect harbour village of Komiža. You'd be forgiven for thinking you were on a movie set in this picturesque place, not least because it's the very same village featured in the 2018 film *Mamma Mia! Here We Go Again*, along with several other locations on the island. I was there for a week, staying in an Airbnb apartment with a balcony that jutted out over the sea. Seven heavenly days were spent exploring the island by foot and on a moped, swimming in the sea, eating delicious fresh seafood, and reading. I don't believe that I enjoyed my week on this enchanting island any less for being there alone.

There is something wonderful about taking off by yourself and being able to do exactly as you please from one minute to the next. Fancy a walk? Good to go. There's no one complaining that they don't feel like exercise and would rather just lie on the beach. Want to get up early to go and watch the sun rise from that amazing vista you were reading about the day before? Done! There's no resistance from a partner who thinks you should be making the most of being able to lie in while you can. Want to be free to stop every three minutes to take an inexplicable number of photos? No problem! There's nobody rushing you because they're bored and irritated by something you happen to be passionate about. Every decision you take,

THRIVE SOLO

every move you make, is yours; every activity is chosen and approved by you; and if you want to eat at the same restaurant by the harbour every night because you've got to know and love both the food and the charming owner, then you bloody well can. No eye rolls or 'you're so borings' to contend with.

It can so often be the case that the person you're travelling with has a very different idea of what fun looks like than you do. Maybe to you, there's nothing more joyous than getting off the beaten track, but your spouse would rather be within walking distance of the nearest McDonald's. Or perhaps your friend is a party animal who wants to stay up drinking until the early hours, whereas you'd rather have early nights so you can make the most of every day. Ultimately, a solo holiday means you don't have to compromise on how you spend your precious time away. It's just pure, unadulterated pleasing of oneself at all times.

Kailee (30, Jacksonville, North Carolina) told me she 'absolutely loved' a trip she took to Japan by herself recently, particularly 'just being able to go to whatever places I wanted. I got to be very spontaneous. I didn't have to plan everything and think about a million other people and factor them in. I basically found a guidebook, picked out all the places I wanted to go to, and just went! It was the coolest experience ever.'

Kaitlin (42, Nashville) is another who absolutely loves to travel by herself for this very reason. When I interviewed her, she had just got back from a solo trip to Italy and had also been to France earlier that year. She said that she simply has 'a much better time when I'm by myself. I can do everything at the pace I want to do it, in order to make my trip the most fun for me. In Italy, my favourite thing was to just be in a city I'd never been [to before], and just take off and wander around. I like to build in time to do completely un-touristy things, like go to thrift stores and flea markets. I can just do, just wander. I love exploring.' She added that: 'I know you can find that in a travel partner, but it's hard. And I think it's different. And the more I travel solo, the more I love it!'

I feel the same, Kaitlin!

Resilience and Self-Discovery

There's a certain sense of self that I, and many of the women I spoke to, gain from solo travel. Whether it was renting a moped in Vis to take on the winding mountain roads, hiring a car to drive all around New England, or simply throwing on a backpack and travelling around East Africa, as I did on my own many years ago, these trips have built up my self-confidence, my resilience, and the belief that I'm capable of doing anything I set my mind to. What's more, all of these attributes have extended far beyond my solo travels and into other aspects of my life.

I remember so clearly on my US road trip feeling somehow more alive than ever before, largely because I was stretching outside of my comfort zone. Although travelling by yourself can push your edges in ways that don't always feel comfortable, the growth that comes on the other side is palpable. This is what makes solo travel one of the best ways to promote independence and self-discovery, not least because it demands that you are truly present with yourself in every moment. And interestingly, a recent study that looked at what motivates people to travel found that it's the transformative experience, freedom and flexibility that drives people to travel alone, as well as the anticipation of self-discovery.[2]

This certainly rings true for Lisa who, as we heard earlier, travelled solo around New Zealand in a camper van for four years. Lisa said that travelling alone makes you 'realise how capable you are, because there's a lot of decision making [and] problem solving, and there's a lot of dealing with new and unfamiliar situations. By being on your own, you *have* to deal with it.'

THRIVE SOLO

Kaitlin (42, Nashville) agrees:

❝ I think it [solo travel] really brings you more awareness of your own resilience. Because when you're travelling and you get thrown a curveball, you need to figure
it out – quickly. You learn something about yourself
every time you go somewhere. It's that idea that, 'OK,
I've got this', you know? I can show up in a new city.
I can navigate this subway. I can get where I need to
go. I just do it. I can bounce back. I can figure stuff out
on the fly. ❞

As travel writer and author Laura Walters (54, Melbourne),
whose quote opened this chapter, told me, travelling alone
will most certainly 'ask of you to dig deep' but 'with all of
the noise gone [of other people], I could really hear what was
going on inside. And in facing a lot of those challenges, I got to
see what I was really capable of as well, and so I got a lot more
confidence in myself.' Her extended alone time meant that she
was able to quiet her mind, which 'created space for another
level of awareness to come to the fore' and it was this space that
allowed her to get clarity about what she wanted from her life.

Kailee (30, Jacksonville, North Carolina) told me that
'being by yourself when you travel gives you so much more
of a feeling of being present – because it's just you, and you're
really connected to your surroundings and what's going on.
You're more immersed in the culture and the experience. So
that's why I really enjoy travelling by myself – just being more
connected with yourself and everything around you because
you're on your own.'

For Annie (44, San Antonio, Texas), solo travel has been a
way of connecting more with nature, too. She said that it took
travelling alone to really help her 'tune into the feeling of nature,
the energy, the vibe, my connection with myself'. I loved what
Annie said about this, and it's something that I resonate with

Solo Travel

very much. When we're alone and we are still – especially in nature – we can begin to truly connect with ourselves and the world around us.

Laura, who has travelled solo extensively, spoke to the joy of independent travel beautifully during our interview for my podcast. In 2013, she walked the Te Araroa trail – a 3000km (1865-mile) route that stretches from Cape Reinga in New Zealand's North Island to Bluff in the South Island – on her own. Here's some of what she shared about the connection she felt in nature:

I was suffering with anxiety and depression just before the trip, and I was not functioning at all. Within a couple of weeks, all of those symptoms that I'd struggled with for over a year were gone. I just suddenly thought, 'Wait a minute, I haven't felt bad for a little while.' And I think it was just the simplicity of life out there. It's kind of like a meditation, so you become very present in the moment, and as the hike went on, I just got very connected with nature, and I felt my human identity falling away – my human story – and I just became part of the greater environment. I really felt part of the earth, and the river, and the sound of the wind in the trees, and my whole identity just fell away. I could listen to who I was inside. I found nature very healing because I felt part of something bigger than me, and it was like an anchor. I find nature like a tuning fork: it's got this energy, and if I can just tune into it, my fragmented, stressed city energy just calms right down. I love it.

As both Laura and Annie said, travelling alone in nature allows us to connect more deeply with ourselves, and it also gives us that sense that there's something greater than ourselves to which we are *always* connected. And there's comfort in that.

99

THRIVE SOLO

Solo Travel Stories

If you're not yet convinced that solo travel is for you, let me finish by sharing with you the words of some women who are planning their first solo trip, some who have found a compromise by travelling solo with others (!), and a couple who describe how fabulous solo travel can really be . . .

Travelling Solo . . . for the First Time

Pip (39, Isle of Wight) has yet to travel abroad alone, but she told me that she plans on booking a solo trip for next year. She has always gone away with girlfriends in the past and loved it, but admitted that there's inevitably always a degree of compromise. She told me that next time, she definitely wants to go away solo, not least because she can find group travel overwhelming and says that she can end up feeling slightly desperate to be on her own. She plans on breaking herself in gently by booking a really nice hotel, which should make things easier.

And Rachel (36, Scotland), who usually prefers to travel with another person, is also planning to make her first ever trip abroad on her own next year – something she says she's always wanted to try. Rachel has done plenty of travel around the UK by herself, but she has only ever travelled overseas with either a friend or a partner. She is currently looking at doing an inter-railing trip, which will involve her spending quite an extended period on her own. Good luck, Rachel!

Travelling Solo . . . with Others

Although solo travel is generally thought of as something that you do entirely alone, it can also be something that you do with other 'solos'. So if you're not quite up to travelling totally on

Solo Travel

your own yet, why not take a leaf out of Jess (42, London) and Lindsey's (45, West Sussex) book?

Jess prefers to travel with other single friends, but when she found herself locked down in London by herself during the pandemic, she forced herself to join a Facebook group of other women who were stuck in London by themselves too. Since then, the Facebook group that was set up to provide support for single women during the pandemic has morphed into a circle of solo women who Jess now travels around the world with. Jess explains:

❝ I've now got this group of six or seven amazing friends. And since then, we've been to Vegas, Miami, Paris, New York and Nice! I've never travelled like it in my life! We'll go to the pub for lunch, and be like, 'Where'd you fancy? Vegas? OK, great, let's book that tomorrow.' Boosh – done! And it just puts such a huge smile on my face knowing that I have this amazing group of women. I just got back from Palma, Majorca, last week. It's just a blessing. It really is. And if you asked, 'What gets the juices flowing for you?', it's being able to do that. I also did Mexico at the beginning of the year. It's just been amazing. And it fills me with so much joy. That's what life is about, right? When you can talk about it and you still get that glow and that smile, that's when you know you're hitting the right spot. **❞**

Lindsey (45, West Sussex) is another who lights up at the thought of travelling, and has visited over 50 countries. While she's travelled extensively by herself, Lindsey also regularly combines travelling alone with seeing other people. At the time of our interview, she was heading off solo to New York for a few days, before being joined by her friend. Lindsey told me that these days she would love to travel alone more, but friends often want to accompany her, especially the ones who

101

THRIVE SOLO

co-parent. She's also planning another 'combination trip' whereby she will travel to the Caribbean alone but visit her friend while she's there.

Travelling Solo . . . Really Can Be Fabulous

Kate and Maddie, who we heard from earlier, have both travelled solo and had a fabulous time. To end on a high, I want to give a little more space to their stories now.

Kate told me that holidaying alone is something she believes she was destined to do from an early age. She talked about the day, aged four, she rode her bike to the end of her street and how this 'massive adventure' felt like 'freedom and independence'. 'I think that was the start of something for me, to be pedalling and to just look behind me and feel a sense of excitement and joy at doing something by myself. And my travels have often been like that.' Kate went on to tell me that after her mum died, she had an overwhelming sense of how short life is, and how she believes it's important to follow your passion and just go out and do what you want to do. One of her greatest joys when it comes to solo holidays is time to simply read:

> ❝ Lying on a beach and having a stack of books is one of life's great joys for me. In regular life, it's quite hard to sit at home and relax with a book when you feel you've got a million things to do. So I stack these books up specifically for trips. The trips are almost like a vehicle for deep reading sessions. And sometimes when I'm lying on the beach with a book, I can disappear into it for four or five hours, and then go to a lovely taverna and eat something, and then go back to the beach and lie down for more reading. You know, it almost doesn't get much better than that. ❞

Kate also told me about the joy she has felt travelling by train around the US, when her 'internal excitement is so big that it was quite hard for me to not just jump up and down in my seat shouting!' She enthused about one train ride from Chicago to New York when she woke up at 6 a.m. and everyone else was asleep. She couldn't get over the fact that she was actually there, and described being 'on the edge of my seat, thrilled and excited, watching, thinking, "Oh my god, I'm in America, I'm on a train. I'm literally living my dream right now. And I've caffeinated myself with a cup of coffee so the dial's gone up to about 120!" But in those moments, I'm just so truly grateful for the capacity to be able to travel and to be able to feel so great about it.'

Maddie told me how much she loved her solo trip to Martha's Vineyard, despite a rather shaky start, which included a migraine and a dead iPhone with no charger. Thankfully, the migraine went, and she managed to find a charger. Maddie explained:

  ❝ I stayed in the same place I'd stayed in when I was 19 – Oak Bluffs. It's just the most beautiful tiny town with dirt roads and wraparound porches. And I just walked down to the beach, and I sat and watched the tide come in and I was like, 'I'm here. I'm actually here.' And I could just walk around with my headphones in, listening to music, looking at everything. I did everything I wanted to do on that trip. I went all around the island. When I went back to Boston, I did a whale watching trip; I did a walking tour; I went up to Salem – I just had the most amazing time. **❞**

Travelling alone gets to be fabulous, and I sincerely hope that if you've never done it, then the stories of the women in this chapter have encouraged and inspired you. It's time to get saving and planning!

THRIVE SOLO

Final Thoughts

We only get one life, and one chance to explore our incredible planet. So we can either continue to wait for a partner to travel the world with us, and that friend of ours to have the time/grown-up kids/money to come with us, or . . . we can take the bull by the horns and go it alone. Because why should we wait?

If you're nervous or apprehensive, why not start with a combination trip, like Lindsey? Or how about a small group tour with one of the many travel agents who are focusing more on solo travellers? Or if you're feeling brave, why not start with somewhere that's not *too* far afield, before venturing on a long-haul trip?

The real question is: will you let fear hold you back, or will you choose to be brave despite the fear? Because one thing is for sure . . . you won't know until you try it, and if nothing else, you will come back with a sense of pride and accomplishment in yourself. And that, my friends, is priceless.

—Podcast Pearls—

'Doing things on your own, although they can be scary, can give you so much more richness and depth of experience. I've had the most amazing and memorable times on my own; some of the times that hold me up when I'm feeling a bit bored or a bit low are the things that I've done by myself – the solo holidays, the solo trips or just solo days out, because you pay so much more attention, and I think life is about paying attention, and choosing where you put that attention.'

— Maddie (50, Bristol)

6

NOT HAVING KIDS

'I am supremely thrilled that I'm not a parent.'

— KAITLIN (42, NASHVILLE)

Fairy tales, parents, friends of parents, the neighbour, the media, the guy in the local fish and chip shop . . . they have all been telling us for centuries that having children is par for the course. It doesn't matter where you come from, where you're going, your upbringing, your education, your job, or what you believe: human beings are expected to have children. Granted, there may be a couple of exceptions – nuns and monks spring to mind – but pretty much everyone comes into this world with their fate (or the expectation of their fate) already sealed in one particular respect: they will be a parent. It's just what you do. What society also tells us is that unless there is a 'valid reason' why we're unable to have children, we will be frowned upon if we either choose not to have children or if we 'end up' not having them.

But this expectation, which has so many of us tripping over ourselves in a bid to live the traditional story, has some glaring omissions. You see, as a society, we've been so preoccupied with the notion that having children *will* be a part of our lives that we've failed to acknowledge – or even discuss – the fact that:

THRIVE SOLO

- Having children can be really, *really* hard and is not always that much fun.

- For some people, a childfree life is their best life.

- There are a significant number of people who actually regret having kids.

And while, of course, for many people, having children *is* the right path, there are also those for whom parenthood is entirely the wrong one. Moreover, some of us non-parents have twigged that life can be equally fabulous (if not more so) without our mini-mes running around the place.

It can almost feel as if there's a secret society of people who have cottoned on to the many freedoms and advantages that come with a childfree existence. But in the meantime, the rest of the world continues to romanticise the raising of tiny humans, often as the only 'acceptable' path, even though the fairy tale often looks a hell of a lot different from the reality. You only need look at various online communities to see that parenthood does not always pan out the way we're led to believe it will.

Now, before we go further, I want to pause for a moment to acknowledge that the focus of this book – as outlined in the introduction – is to celebrate the wonderful things about being single and childfree in and of themselves. The purpose of this book is not, therefore, to use the downsides of being part of a couple with kids as the means for highlighting the upsides of singledom. (After all, solo life is intrinsically a full and valid existence, and it doesn't require the lambasting of its coupled counterpart to validate or justify its inherent worth.)

However, when discussing children, the ingrained narrative that tells us a childless life is 'less than' is so pervasive that in this instance it's almost impossible to talk about the benefits of a childfree life without drawing comparisons to the life of a parent. This chapter will, therefore, very much focus on the less-than-ideal aspects of parenthood as a means of defending a childfree life, and it'll be putting the spotlight on some of the reasons why *not* having children might be the best thing that some of us could ever *not* do – whether by choice, circumstance or otherwise. So, back to where we were . . .

Even a very brief look at the 'regretfulparents' page on Reddit[1] (which at the time of writing has 121k members) shows subject lines such as:

- 'I can't do this any more'
- 'Prison'
- 'I never wanted this'
- 'I ruined my life'

One mother, known as Tammy, wrote anonymously for the feminist website *The Vagenda* that: 'It seems as though your entire self becomes nothing more than a functional enabler for your kids' success.'[2] I don't know about you, but this doesn't sound particularly appealing to me.

One of the women I spoke to was Maddie (50, Bristol), who quoted to me a line from the 2023 *Barbie* movie: 'We mothers stand still so our daughters can look back to see how far they've come.'[3] Maddie's response?

❝ Well, that sounds really shit. Why should they have to? I understand what they're getting at, and I understand maybe that's how it feels to be a mother, basically sacrificing all of your wants and needs and desires and autonomy so that these other beings can thrive. But when did we decide that that level of selflessness was the only good way to be as a woman? Because men don't have to do that. ❞

She makes a good point.

Israeli sociologist Orna Donath published a study in 2015 based on interviews she carried out with 23 Israeli mothers

THRIVE SOLO

who regret having had children. Donath concluded from her findings that while motherhood 'may be a font of personal fulfilment, pleasure, love, pride, contentment and joy', it 'may simultaneously be a realm of distress, helplessness, frustration, hostility and disappointment, as well as an arena of oppression and subordination'.[4] Yet somehow the harsh realities of parenthood remain hidden behind the perfect Instagram photo, or the weight of shame that women feel when they admit to themselves – let alone to anyone else – that motherhood is not necessarily as joyous a journey as they had expected.

As a society, we're so brainwashed by the notion that being a parent is, without exception, a 'wonderful' experience (and the inevitable icing on the cake of our adult lives) that there's no room for those women who struggle or regret having kids to share how they *truly* feel. (Hence the anonymous Reddit group online.)

Yet the truth is that having kids can make some women feel as though they've lost themselves, that their lives are no longer their own, and that they're living a life of servitude. They can also feel that they've sacrificed the things that *they* wanted, that their freedom has been stolen from them, and that they're desperate for alone time. And in some cases, while of course they love their children, they may not actually *like* them for any of the above reasons. Because, let's face it, just because we give birth to a child, there's no guarantee we're going to necessarily like the human being they become.

What we're missing in the current narrative is an acknowledgement that being a parent is by no means for everyone; and more than that, an acknowledgement that having children can have a hugely negative impact on some of the most wonderful aspects of life: time, peace and quiet, freedom, sleep, a clean and tidy home, and space for oneself. Sure, it's expected that parents will have to sacrifice certain things when they embark

Not Having Kids

upon child-rearing, but these sacrifices are brushed off far too flippantly, as if they're unimportant. They're not.

Neither desiring nor loving motherhood are biological predispositions for all women. And while society tends to divide non-mothers into the two extremes of 'didn't want them' or 'couldn't have them', there is much nuance within this topic. I myself do not fall at either end of that spectrum, but somewhere in the messy middle. One of my wonderful podcast guests, Ruby Warrington, spoke to this when she talked about the idea that 'either it's a tragedy that you can't have kids, or you're cold and selfish because you don't want kids.' The truth is that the reasons for women not having kids are so vastly varied that it's almost impossible to put any of them into one particular category. And just as nobody's life story is black and white, neither are the stories of those women who do not have children.

A look at some of the research into happiness and parenthood confirms that having children is an experience far more multifarious than society and cultural expectation would have us believe. Several studies conducted in recent years by sociologist Robin Simon have shown that parents actually report lower levels of happiness and higher levels of depressive symptoms, as well as poorer physical health, than non-parents.[5] In addition, studies published in the journal *Psychological Science* show that it's women who are bearing the brunt of this stress and unhappiness, and that it's the dads who may report higher levels of happiness.[6]

In the first half of this chapter we'll be exploring why having kids isn't necessarily all it's cracked up to be, and then in the second part we'll be looking at the different paths in life that are more easily available for non-mothers.

Part One: Having Kids Is Hard

There's a reason why people refer to motherhood as the hardest job in the world. We've all seen it, haven't we? The hungover friend in actual hell while juggling a toddler with the overwhelming need to vomit; the look of exasperation on the face of the mother whose teenage son has just slammed the door and stormed out of the house; the frustration on the face of the colleague bemoaning the fact that she never has a moment to herself any more; or the anxiety of your bestie who's worried that she might have fucked her kid up already because of that thing she said when she lost her cool the other night. Whichever way you slice it, being a mother ain't easy.

The fabulous, funny and straight-talking TV presenter Bev Turner – also a previous guest on my podcast – told me in the way only she can about the realities of having children (she has three). Referring to herself and other mothers as 'we burdened women', Bev explained how she was 'just born broody. I bought baby clothes before I was even married. Then I had my first child, and now we get down to the reality of the situation. I had bought into the pro-natal industry hook, line and sinker. I couldn't get over the fact that, as modern women, we'd been sold this idea that motherhood would be easy.' If this is the case, then it stands to reason that some of us might at the very least hesitate before diving into motherhood, if not choose to avoid it altogether. Which is what the women below say.

Kate (55, London), who knew from early on in life that she didn't want kids, has observed how hard being a parent can be through the various people in her life who *are* married with kids:

> ❝ I've seen it up close with my friends: compromises that people have to make; how it is having small children, trying to have a life, trying to have it all. It is fucking hard. I see women I work with trying to progress their careers and manage their families. And it's

Not Having Kids

hard work. I just wasn't sure I was cut out for that – I knew I wasn't. 🎝🎝

Another woman who concluded she didn't want kids of her own, having observed how hard it was for the families around her, is Jean (67, Clearwater, Florida). Jean told me that she used to babysit regularly for multiple children when she was a teenager. She began by looking after a five-year-old girl, and subsequently babysat for three sets of twins and another family with seven children. Her experience from the age of 12 until 21 of looking after other people's children drove her decision to not have her own.

Kaitlin (42, Nashville) and Kerri (51, Brisbane) both expressed their perceptions around how hard it can be to bring up children. While Kerri absolutely loves being an auntie, she told me that she's always 'itching to get home' after a visit because in her words, 'it's relentless'. Kaitlin simply said that in her opinion being a parent is 'too fucking hard. That's the thing. It's just too fucking hard.' When I asked her what she meant by 'too hard' she replied, 'I like my life. I like the ease. I like the spontaneity. I like the simplicity', and these are all things that Kaitlin feels would change if she had children.

Each stage of motherhood has its own, unique blend of hardness, whether it be the sleepless newborn days, the 'terrible two' toddler days, the monosyllabic teenager days, or the lost and confused twenty-something days. And there is no denying that they all come with anxieties, disappointments, frustrations and heartaches, which, as my own mother has pointed out to me more than once, never go away. I've witnessed several friends go through extremely tough times with their kids – from mental health issues to behavioural problems. My own sister has four children who, much as she adores them, have caused her worries that I've observed with the opposite of envy. If anything, watching those closest to me on their journeys of

THRIVE SOLO

parenthood has only confirmed my status as 'childfree' rather than 'childless' (see p. 9) – despite my previous ambivalence around having kids.

I personally had always assumed that having kids of my own would just sort of . . . happen. Somewhere down the line. There were opportunities when I could have settled down with two or three of my former long-ish-term boyfriends, but I walked away knowing instinctively that the relationships weren't right for me, and that the pull of maternal desire simply wasn't strong enough. The idea of staying in a relationship that didn't feel right, primarily to have a baby, was never an option; and besides, until I hit my 40s, the tick of my biological clock was so quiet that I could barely make it out. The 'broodiness' that my friends referred to was completely lost on me, and I wondered why I simply couldn't relate to something that seemed to be so clearly alive and kicking (pun intended) in seemingly every other woman on the planet. But then in the years since turning 40, the clock that had for so long remained silent finally started making up for its lack of sound by not just ticking, but shattering the silence with its alarm.

There followed a few years during which I silently grieved that, in all likelihood, the motherhood ship had left the harbour and sailed away from me for good. But even in that window of time, when I could have potentially still made it happen, I did not. And as I travelled further into my forties and became more fully aware of how hard parenthood was, any sadness was replaced with the realisation that *not* having a child afforded me no end of opportunities and freedoms.

So, we've established that being a parent is hard, but let's look a bit more closely at exactly *why* this is the case.

The Burden of Responsibility Is Heavy

As a parent, gov.uk states, your main parental responsibilities are to provide a home for your child, protect and maintain your child, discipline your child, choose and provide for their education, agree to their medical treatment, and look after their property.[7] This official guidance does not, of course, touch on the many other responsibilities of catering to your child's every need. Off the top of my head, a few other things parents have to manage are:

- children's changing moods;
- dealing with toddler tantrums;
- driving them to every sports game, birthday party, sleepover and other activity;
- ensuring homework gets done (always one I'm genuinely grateful not to have to partake in);
- making sure they clean their teeth every night and morning;
- policing social media/internet activity to make sure they're not being brainwashed or groomed (thank you, Lord, for sparing me from the anxiety of this particular shitshow);
- cajoling them into studying for college-entrance exams;
- attending parents' evenings (aren't the days long enough?);
- going to (let's face it, crap) school plays;
- teaching your child to be a good person (no pressure);
- holding them accountable for their mistakes;

THRIVE SOLO

- ensuring that your child goes off into the world as an independent, happy, kind, caring, successful, decent human;

- always setting a good example yourself.

Seriously, I need to lie down.

The overwhelming and profound responsibility of being a parent must surely be one of the most difficult tasks. And the list above is just about *one* child. Imagine if there were two, or three, or – help! – four or more . . . My own mum has described parenthood as a 'never-ending sense of responsibility', which, to put it mildly, 'can be trying'. Sorry, Mum.

On the 'regretfulparents' page from reddit.com that I mentioned earlier, one person talked of how they were 'dying inside due to the pressure and responsibility' of parenthood, while another wrote about being 'so mentally tired of feeling trapped with being a parent and the responsibility it entails'. Just the thought of this almost unfathomable amount of obligation that a parent has to their child makes me feel stressed. And there's really no escaping it. Even being responsible for the safety, well-being and happiness of my beloved cat can sometimes feel like too much. But an actual *human*? Here's what Drea (38, North East England), a fellow happily childfree woman, had to say about it:

❝ When I think about my friends with kids, I genuinely get anxiety. You know, the freedom of just not having that level of responsibility. You are essentially committing yourself to those children for the rest of their lives. It's not to 18; it's literally for the rest of their lives. You need to help them get through things, and goodness knows what's going to happen in their lives. The world is not a wonderful, safe place all of the time. It just makes me feel really tense, and I think if you're going to make that decision, you've got to be so

Not Having Kids

sure – you've got to be so sure of yourself. For me, the pressure and the level of responsibility and stress and anxiety would be too much. 🗦🗦

Karen (51, London), who, like me, is childless by circumstance (see p. 120), summarised her own feelings wonderfully:

🗧🗧 I – like so many other women out there – assumed that I would have children at some point in my future, although it was never my driving force in life. I was far too distracted with just living, and when all my friends started having babies around me, I remember finding it all rather strange, surreal, and certainly not something I was in any hurry to do. By the time I found myself single at 40, I assumed the baby ship had probably sailed; but the funny thing was that I actually felt relieved, because almost without realising it, I'd got to a point in my life where the thought of taking on the responsibility of a child was completely unimaginable. The truth is that the enormous weight of being 100 per cent responsible for another human being, and being expected to put its needs before your own, isn't something that gets talked about [enough] considering the massive intrusion into a person's life that it actually is! I know that sounds awful, but having a child is a huge encumbrance on anyone's life. That doesn't negate you loving them to pieces; it's simply a fact, whichever way you look at it. 🗦🗦

Karen makes a compelling point. But thanks to the equally compelling narrative we've all grown up with – the expectation that as women we will have children without question and without complaint – we fail to explore the many built-in consequences of actually having them. Many of us don't examine thoroughly the impact that this life-altering event might have

THRIVE SOLO

on our world, preferring instead to follow the stipulated guidelines of life laid out for us long before we were even a twinkle in our own parents' eyes.

To make parenting even harder, children these days are increasingly experiencing mental health issues, which adds to parents' already heavy load in sometimes truly crushing ways. According to UK charity the Children's Society, the likelihood of young people having a mental health problem has increased by 50 per cent in the last three years: 52 per cent of 17- to 23-year-olds have experienced a deterioration in mental health in the last five years, and one in six children aged 5 to 16 are likely to have a mental health problem.[8] The same trend is seen elsewhere in the world, from the US to Australia. For example, a survey from the Australian Psychological Society has found a 'shocking increase' in mental health issues in children ranging from 18 months to 18 years of age. In the 6- to 12-year-old group, there has been a 'sharp rise in several mental illnesses and symptoms with Social Anxiety Disorder (45%), ADHD (42%), peer relationship difficulties (39%), problematic screen use (36%), and educational learning concerns (35%) the five largest increases.'[9] And of 'particular concern' is the increase in both Generalised Anxiety Disorder and Autism Spectrum Disorder among 18-month to 5-year-olds.

As a non-parent, it's difficult to comprehend the worry and struggle that would go alongside having a neurotypical child with stable mental health, let alone a child struggling with any of the above difficulties. This is something that Gina (55, Los Angeles) mentioned during our conversation. And as a natural worrier myself, who frequently goes into a tailspin when my cat disappears for more than a few hours, I very much related to Gina's perspective when she shared the following:

> ❝ I just don't think I would've been able to manage my anxiety [if I were a parent]. Ever since Covid, I keep joking with people that there's never been a better

Not Having Kids

time to not have children. Covid, climate change, just the overpowering anxiety of having children. I feel like I have spent the past three years of my life being a sounding board for [my friends] because they're going through the hell of 'I feel like my child is not in a safe place.' And I know many people who have kids with special needs. So again, the fantasy is always that you're married and there's never any problems in your marriage, and your kids are all happy and healthy . . . and that's not the reality for people. 🥢🥢

Gina went on to say that she believes that the one group of people who 'never feel sorry for the single ladies' is women with very young children. She talked of a time when she was able to take off to Italy at a moment's notice with a hot guy she'd met, and how envious of her women with small children were. She acknowledged the load these women were bearing, and how hard motherhood so clearly is, and felt grateful for her own situation.

I'm now going to delve more deeply into two of the main downsides of motherhood that women with – in particular, small – children often speak about: boredom and a loss of a sense of self.

Boredom

Make no mistake: there are certain aspects of parenting that are, not to put too fine a point on it, dull as shit. Particularly in those early years. And repeatedly doing boring things is hard. When I imagine a parallel life in which I'm married with kids, I shudder at the thought of having to spend my time playing make-believe tea parties while sipping from a non-existent cup, listening to my child trying to read the word 'cat' and suppressing the urge to yell 'for fuck's sake, it's so easy!', watching

THRIVE SOLO

Peppa Pig for the 794th time and pretending not to want to be absolutely anywhere else.

Karen (51, London) and I are singing from the same hymn sheet. She told me:

> **"** One of the things I'm so grateful I don't have to deal with is all of the moments of boredom that come with parenting. I've heard so many friends talk about how much they loathe 'bath and bedtime', how they resent the constant food preparation that seems to drive them to distraction, and how sometimes they want to cry as they wander around the house tidying up after their kids of varying ages. I know myself, and I'm not sure I would've coped with the monotony of it. Because in many ways it's a life of monotony, no doubt about it. **"**

I also want to share something from Bella DePaulo (70, Summerland, California), who put this so beautifully:

> **"** I once stopped by the home of a woman who was there with her four-year-old son, and he was absolutely adorable. He was sitting at the kitchen table with this colouring book; he looked very contented and very engaged in his colouring. There was sunlight coming in from the window behind him, and it sort of bathed him in this golden glow. If you wanted to create an ad for the appeal of parenting, that would be it. I mean, it was amazing. But what I felt was if I had to switch places with that mother, I would go stark, raving mad. To me, that wasn't a picture of the joys of parenting or the fulfilment of having a kid. It was a picture of boredom. So I think it's things like that that inform me of what it means to me not to have kids. It means that even under the best of circumstances, it's not what I want. I don't want that to be my life. **"**

Bella's words resonated with me. Much as I think my friends' kids are sweet and lovely, I do not envy the moments of 'kid activities' that they are forced to take part in, or the tedium of relentlessly doing the same thankless tasks day in, day out. I cannot think of anything more yawnsome.

Loss of Your Sense of Self

TV presenter Bev Turner, who I mentioned on p. 110, spoke to surely one of the hardest things about having and raising kids: the sense of losing yourself. Bev told me that she'd entered the world of motherhood with the idea that she would be 'writing books, with children playing around my feet'. But as she admitted, this idea was somewhat nuts. She explained to me how she had moments of asking herself, 'What have I done? How do I claim my identity? How do I keep who I am while still loving and caring for these children in the best possible way?' and added that 'there is always a little sliding door in my head, like "what if?"' Bev went on to tell me about a time recently when she happened to have the whole house to herself and, funnily enough, she asked herself, 'What would Lucy do?' As she happily read an essay, drank some delicious wine and ate some lovely food, she remembered who she is and what makes her happy.

As Bev's story shows, raising children is relentless, and the reality can often bear little or no resemblance to the stories we've all grown up with. While there's no doubt that many wonderful things can come from motherhood, the risk of losing oneself was a recurring concern among the women I spoke to. This often manifests as mothers putting others first to such an extent that it's like they almost cease to exist – the constant demands and lack of gratitude causing their personalities to morph to fit the expected mould of 'mother' or 'partner'.

THRIVE SOLO

This is a consolation for those of us who are free from such encumbrance and can rest easy in the knowledge that our sense of self remains intact – at least as far as not being a mother is concerned. For me personally, I know that the feeling that my identity was slipping away from me would have been one of the aspects of parenthood that I would have struggled with.

Part Two: A Different Path

Not that I likely need convince most readers of this book, but let's put to rest the misguided notion that every woman out there wants kids. They don't. And while I'm at it, let me add that neither is every childless or childfree woman missing out on the only 'real' love that exists in this universe. Also not the case. Although women without kids undeniably miss out on the experience of loving and being loved by their own child, to suggest that this is the 'most important' or 'most meaningful' kind of love is both patronising and incredibly narrow-minded. Aside from anything else, you don't know what you don't know, and the swathes of happily single, childfree women I've come across, joyfully living their freedom-filled lives, don't seem too upset about the absence of this particular kind of love – myself included. In this world of 8 billion people, it stands to reason that at least *some* of those people are simply on a different path. In this section, I'll be looking at a few of the many different situations that can lead us to not having kids, as well as the benefits and opportunities these paths can offer us.

Childfree through Circumstance

I don't remember the exact moment when I truly understood that I had not been put on this earth to become a mother. I'd had an inkling since my thirties, although back then it was buried underneath the assumption that I would *of course* have kids, eventually. But somewhere between Covid-19 and hearing about the perils of homeschooling, and starting a podcast about celebrating 'spinsters' – both of which brought about an understanding that there was *so* much more to life than kids – I realised that I had, in fact, always known that my destiny was not to be a mother, and that I was actually here to share and promote a different kind of love with the world: the self variety. Plus, of course, I simply hadn't met the right partner.

The point is that not every woman is meant to be a mother, and those of us who aren't have just as much to contribute to the world as those who are. For many of us, the lightbulb moment comes once we have acknowledged our circumstances and realised that perhaps, after all, we won't have the children we once thought we might. Kate (55, London), who is also childfree primarily because of circumstance, has this to say on the matter:

> ❝ I had a moment in my early 40s, dating like a demon, trying to meet a man I could have children with. I had a lot of fun, but it also felt hard, running against a clock that I could hear ticking. One day, sitting on my bed, I had the sudden thought that maybe that isn't the path for me and maybe I'm not here for that. I had the very clear and incredibly calming realisation that we are all here to do different things – that some of the things we thought we'd do, we won't, and that that's OK. Everything changed in that moment. My perspective shifted and I stopped trying to force something and just flowed with what I felt pulled to do. ❞

Lindsey (45, West Sussex) told me that she'd always had 'the deepest desire to fall in love and potentially meet somebody in time to think about having a child together' but that that didn't happen for her. She said that she tried everything

THRIVE SOLO

in terms of dating and felt awful when relationships didn't progress because she knew that 'not only was I then losing that desire for falling in love and having that companionship in a romantic partner, but also as I was getting older, the clock was ticking, and I knew I was also losing another potential – to have a child with that person.' For many years, Lindsey felt devastated that her circumstances hadn't enabled her to be a mother, and then when she turned 43 her 'dark day of reckoning came' and she subsequently visited a fertility clinic to find out how she might go about having a child on her own. However, when she actually started exploring the process of solo motherhood, she realised that despite it having been 'hammered into' her that a child would bring her happiness, she actually didn't want to do it alone. So she didn't, and she now has no regrets about that choice.

To help her get to this place of acceptance, Lindsey found a coach whom she worked with intensively over a significant period of time, delving deep into the 'inner work'. In time, she was able to identify, process and flip the script on many of the subconscious beliefs that had been telling her for so long that not having children was pitiful and shameful. Lindsey explained:

> **❝** This change didn't happen overnight – it took months. I broke down, and I cried, and I let the grief out when I realised that I was never going to be a mum. But that was not my path. And I quickly got over it – really quickly. And I think actually, deep down, it was the conditioning. And even though I know I would've been a fantastic mother, because I've got a fantastic mother who is so maternal, and I carry a maternal energy with me, I actually don't think it was my path. **❞**

Other women are childfree through a mixture of circumstance and choice. An example of this is Pip (39, Isle of Wight), who told me that having children 'would be the absolute opposite of anything that I would ever want to do'. Pip went through premature menopause when she was just 15 years old and says that she feels like her life was shaped by this. Understandably, she has wondered whether this is the reason for her never wanting kids.

❝ I'm technically childless, but what's weird is I don't know if it's because of that [experiencing premature menopause] or if it's because of who I am as a person. I've never in my life felt affected by that. I think I was one of those people who knew from a little tiny kid that I was never going to have a baby. It's never once affected me, really. Never once have I thought 'I want a baby.' Not once in my life. I look at babies and I don't get it. I literally don't get it. I might as well be looking at a bag of peas! ❞

Lindsey, Kate, Pip and I are testament to the fact that it's possible to end up not having children – partially through circumstance – but still go on to live a happy life without them. There are so many different reasons why a woman may end up without kids, or difficulties that prevent it from happening – issues with fertility, financial constraints, a partner who doesn't want children. Whatever the particular circumstance looks like for you, it's possible to reach a place where you can feel grateful that it didn't happen for you, because you're *meant* to be on a different path.

Childfree through Choice

Let's hear now from some women who actively chose not to walk the path of parenthood. Women like Ileana (38, Northern California), who shared that 'I feel like sometimes people imagine it to be this passive, accidental type thing that happens, and

THRIVE SOLO

not an active choice that we're not making every, single day. I feel like I choose on a daily basis to not pursue partnership and to not pursue motherhood.' She adds that: 'Sometimes I'll be somewhere people are maybe struggling with children, or their relationship, and while I really empathise, and I appreciate that, at the same time I'm thinking to myself "I'm so glad that I made this choice."' Ileana also told me that she's 'done a lot of soul searching about it, and I've really examined myself and the societal pressure to be partnered and to have children'. She has concluded that 'I don't agree with those. I don't think that pressure should be put on any woman. And I'm in a position to make a choice here, and so I'm going to do it.'

Jess (42, London) has known for a long time that kids aren't for her:

> ❝ I knew I didn't want kids very early on. I think that's just been a thing that's always been there. It's never been my journey. It's never been my path. It's just not within my DNA, I guess. It's one of those things that I just knew. There was no argument, there was no debate on it – that was just me. [. . .] I think I knew from probably my late teens, early twenties. And I'm good with it because it's opened up so many other doors to go out there and explore life [. . .] and I'm just going to enjoy that and revel in that. I love it. ❞

The same is true for Cerian (39, Dijon, Spain), who told me: 'Even when I was little, I always remember thinking, no, I don't want kids. I can't actually think of anything worse than having kids and being married. And the kids thing was weird because it took me a long time to feel OK with saying [it]. When I was in my late twenties and early thirties, I used to really feel like there was something wrong with me for not feeling maternal. But that was probably just from pressure I was getting from my ex-husband's family and stuff. And now I feel totally fine with it.'

Many other women echo these stories, and none of them feels any regret or sadness, because each one of them has chosen to be on a different path.

Saving the Planet

Like many other childfree women, Rachel (36, Scotland) loves children, but is still very clear that she doesn't want her own. However, her reasons for remaining childfree are different to those we've heard so far. I'll let Rachel explain:

❝ I love children – I love my niece, and my friends' children as well. And I think I can be a good auntie and role model to them, so that's how I look at it. I love other people's children and, you know, that's enough for me. I've decided that I don't want my own children for a few reasons, but largely from an environmental perspective. I just feel that it's not going to benefit the planet, and I wouldn't want to bring a child into a potentially uncertain future, so there's a moral side to it as well. The population is already huge, and probably more than the earth can accommodate. So I'm willing to sacrifice not having a child for that. We've got a limited amount of resources, and humans are already consuming more than they should. **❞**

Rachel's environmental reasons for remaining childfree bring into question the narrative that tells us childfree women are 'selfish' (see p. 25). As Pip (39, Isle of Wight) says, 'I can't bear the selfish narrative. I just think that if we all had babies, this world probably wouldn't exist now, because if we did all have them, then there's a much bigger problem, isn't there?'

THRIVE SOLO

Back in 2023, I welcomed on to the podcast Nandita Bajaj, Executive Director at Population Balance, an organisation whose vision is 'a future where our human footprint is in balance with life on Earth, enabling all species to thrive', and whose mission is to 'inspire narrative, behavioural, and system change that shrinks our human impact and elevates the rights and well-being of people, animals, and the planet'. What follows is a lengthy quote from Nandita, which I thought was important to share in its entirety. As an expert in her field, she makes some crucial and valid points about a sensitive topic that perhaps doesn't always get the airtime it should:

> ❝ Scientists would call the state that we're in 'ecological overshoot', which means that we are basically extracting and taking away the gifts and services that earth provides way faster than it can regenerate. And the earth obviously can, and has been able to, regenerate for millennia. And we've been able to live in balance for a very long time. But we're at a point – I think we hit that point about 50 years ago – where earth is no longer able to keep up with our demands. And so we've been in a constant state of overshoot – it's like we're living off our credit card, earth's credit card. A good way of looking at it is that we are living off our principle, not our interest. And ecological overshoot is both a product of how quickly we are growing in our numbers, but also how much we are consuming. So both our population and our consumption are trending upwards. Scientists are saying that a stable population or sustainable population at, let's say, a sustainable level of consumption, would be anywhere from 2 to 4 billion. And we just hit 8 billion a couple of months ago in November [2022].
>
> So we are far higher than where we should be. And that has resulted in a lot of crises: ecological crises, but

also social crises, ecological being the most common; the one we hear about the most is climate crisis. The biodiversity crisis is the second main one, which doesn't get talked about enough. And that's basically losing species at an alarmingly high rate. And that's absolutely in concert with what we call human expansionism. [. . .] As we are growing, we're crowding out all of the other species in a way that has not happened before with any other species. We've kind of just taken this human supremacist worldview where we, through our technology, through our energy, through, you know, our kind of domination capacity, have slowly taken over much of the ice-free land. And there's really no aspect, no part of the planet that we haven't touched, that remains pristine. And we are completely intertwined with our earth. We're not separate from it. We believe we are.

So all of those ecological crises are then feeding into and fuelling a lot of the social crises, the social crises being, of course, resource scarcity, climate-caused displacement. So people are having to leave homes and migrate to places that are not their home. And all sorts of other political unrest, social unrest, etc. And one aspect of what we look at is that the driver of population growth is pronatalism – this unchecked pressure put on people to have children. **"**

Nandita went on to tell me a little bit about the history of a child's place in society. This was following a conversation she'd had with Orna Donath – the sociologist I mentioned earlier in this chapter – who carried out the study on mothers who regret having children (see p. 107). Nandita shared how Orna talked about how we used to be a more agricultural society before we became so heavily urbanised. Children were needed to work

THRIVE SOLO

on farms, so people tended to have a lot of them in order to survive. Nandita said this about what she learned from Orna:

> ❝ Someone figured out that to keep making people have kids, we had to attach this emotional significance to kids. So historically you don't hear as many depictions of kids being these little angels, as having this really strong emotional sort of aura around them. That was something that's been perpetuated through the media, through our culture somehow, to ensure that people have large families. And so through this process of work of being exposed to all the research, and doing a lot of reading ourselves, some researchers have suggested that there's a latent desire for women to have small families. That most women, if you sort of peel away all these layers of pronatalism – and there are so many as we're starting to talk about them, from the economy, from the tax credits that we get for each child, from every TV series, every movie we watch, [which] sort of depicts the families with children as being more whole, as being more fulfilled, as having this veneer of completion. [. . .] It's very hard for people to know what they really want. But there's some suggestion in cultures where people do suddenly get more access to contraception, for example, [of] societal attitudes start[ing] to change. Where women have more access to education, where they're more liberated from the demands of their husbands, fertility magically declines pretty much everywhere. ❞

Clearly, broaching the subject of having fewer children, or no children, in order to save the planet is an extremely sensitive and complex subject, and not one that there's space here to go into in any detail. But it is impossible to ignore the fact that our desire to procreate to the extent that we do – not to

Not Having Kids

mention the weight of societal expectation that drives many who would rather *not* have kids to have them – has huge and potentially devastating consequences for our planet (without which we wouldn't be able to exist at all, let alone reproduce!). It's also worth pondering whether people might consider smaller families, as well as musing on the question of whether it is in fact ethical to bring even one child, let alone multiple children, into the world when the future of our planet is so uncertain. Miley Cyrus told *Elle* magazine that we're 'getting handed a piece-of-s*** planet, and I refuse to hand that down to my child',[10] and a 2020 YouGov poll found that 'nearly one in eleven (9 per cent) adults who don't have kids say they were concerned that the planet is already overpopulated and 5 per cent say they worried about the impact having children would have on climate change and the environment.'[11] I can imagine that number will only continue to grow.

In 2019, congresswoman Alexandria Ocasio-Cortez, who at the time of writing has 8.2 million followers on Instagram, asked a highly contentious question on social media that made waves. Talking about how millennials are choosing to be childless because of the climate crisis, she said that it 'is basically a scientific consensus that the lives of our children are going to be very difficult, and it does lead young people to have a legitimate question: is it OK to still have children?'[12]

An article in *The Guardian*, also in 2019, looked at the work of BirthStrike. The brainchild of Blythe Pepino, Birth-Strike is a voluntary organisation for both women and men who've decided not to have kids because of the coming 'climate breakdown and civilisation collapse'.[13] Pepino herself had 'this overwhelming urge to create a family' with her partner, Joshua, but said that she 'couldn't bring myself to do it'. As the article says, she found that 'other women – especially those

THRIVE SOLO

in climate-conscious circles – were struggling with the same question' as Ocasio-Cortez, 'but were "too afraid to talk about it" for fear of judgement or ridicule'.

It's hardly surprising that people are frightened to admit their feelings on such a controversial topic, but we also need to ask ourselves why an 'admission' about a conscious choice to remain childless due to the dire state of our planet should cause any shame or reprimand, when it is abundantly clear there's a valid argument that deserves to be given voice.

Final Thoughts

We've heard from multiple women in this chapter – women who wanted kids but due to circumstance and/or a combination of factors didn't have them, and women who simply chose not to. But whatever *your* reasons for not becoming a mother, the many benefits of remaining childfree are clear. Despite the undeniably wonderful things about having kids, there are an equal amount of things that are *not* wonderful, and it can be all too easy to romanticise the former and understate the latter.

We mustn't downplay the genuine difficulties and challenges of being a parent, just as we mustn't underrate the blessings of a childfree life. So, the next time you're walking through town on a Saturday afternoon, bring your attention to the faces of those parents who are clearly *not* loving parenthood. Notice the furrowed brows as they trail around behind their offspring, the look of frustration at the tantrum in the supermarket aisle, or the flash of resentment in their eyes that betrays a desire to be somewhere else, doing something else. And take a moment to feel grateful that you are not them and embrace your childfree status with pride and pleasure.

—Podcast Pearls—

'[Having kids] was always something I just presumed that one day I would want, but that day never came. It's the lifestyle – it's not the kids, and I want to make that very clear because lots of people assume that if you don't want kids, you don't like kids. I love kids. But it's the lifestyle that I never wanted, and honestly, as I've got older, I've just got surer of that decision! Of course there is a little semblance of doubt; you think "Will I one day regret this?" because everyone tells you, you know, one day you'll regret this. But I am just *so* sure that it was the right decision.'

— Helen (47, Brighton)

7

SEX

'For all the effort, I honestly can't be arsed.'

— KERRI (51, BRISBANE)

At the time of writing, in early 2024, I have not had sex since July 2020; and before that I hadn't had sex since October 2017. And for more context, the sex I had in 2020 came out of a fling (if you could call it that), meaning it only happened on a few occasions. So, if you put that brief dalliance aside, I basically have not had sex for nearly seven years. There, I said it. Should I be ashamed to admit this? Should I pretend that I'm getting it regularly despite having been single for years? Or should I just tell it like it is, knowing that the truth will set me free, and that being brutally honest means there's nothing to hide, which, frankly, makes life easier? Either way, I'll tell you something even more inexplicable: I don't miss it. Say, what?!

Before you get all up in arms, thinking to yourself, 'Well, she's clearly never had great sex then', let me give you some more context. I was a pretty sexual person from my teenage years when I first entered the world of shagging. Sex was something I greatly enjoyed and had quite a lot of, with quite a lot of blokes, from the age of 15 (I know, the shame!) to the age of 41. It was always just, well, a part of my life – until, that is, the dawning of the Age of Celibacy, which arrived without warning. But despite all of this, and to reiterate what I stated in the previous

THRIVE SOLO

paragraph, I honestly don't miss it – 99 per cent of the time. The only time I actually *do* think about sex and feel like it might be quite nice to have some of it, is when I'm watching a sex scene in a film or something on Netflix. In those moments, I try to avert my eyes and wish for it to be over quickly so that I can go back into a state of 'out of sight, out of mind'.

But that's just me. In this chapter, I'm going to share what I think the reasons might be behind my personal not-giving-a-shit-about-not-having-sex mentality. I'll then tell you what some of the single women I interviewed had to say about sex – their thoughts on it, whether they're getting it, and whether or not they miss it. I was intrigued to find out whether it's just me who doesn't seem particularly bothered by my current lack of sexual activity. But before that, let's have a brief look at what seems to be going on in the wider world when it comes to sex, such as its benefits, and how many people are having it – and how often.

Sex Stats

Research shows that sexual activity comes with a range of benefits – not least keeping the human race going (let's disregard the case for a childfree life for a moment). A 2023 article in *MedicalNewsToday* suggests that those benefits include reduced blood pressure, improved mood, a reduction in stress, improved sleep, and even a protective effect on cardiovascular health.[1] The Oregon Health & Science University Center for Women's Health lists the further benefits of improved self-esteem, decreased depression and anxiety, and immediate, natural pain relief.[2] So, sex is good for both our physical and mental health, but how many of us are actually having it?

In the UK, a 2019 report in the *British Medical Journal*, which surveyed data from over 34,000 men and women aged 16 to 44 years old, found that fewer than half of British men

Sex

and women have sex at least once a week, and that the number of people having sex declined between 2001 and 2012.[3] This decline was apparent across all age groups for women (and all but one for men), but the most notable and steepest decline was among those aged 25 and over, and those who were married or cohabiting. The findings also show that nearly a third of men and women have not had sex in the past month. And, that the 'number of occasions of sex in the past month fell from four to two among 35- to 44-year-old women, and from four to three among men in this age group'. In other words, if you're a woman between the ages of 35 and 44, you're only on average having sex twice a month. There is also UK data from YouGov showing that 'increasing numbers of people give up sex completely as they get older. Almost a fifth of 40- to 44-year-olds don't have sex at all. By 74, this figure jumps to 57 per cent.'[4] Even Robbie Williams, who has just turned 50 at the time of writing, has declared that he and his wife aren't doing it either. I don't feel so bad now.

As for the state of sex in the US – people are having less sex than they were a decade ago, whether they're in their teens or in their forties. A comprehensive sex study from the National Survey of Sexual Health and Behavior showed a decline between 2009 and 2018 in all forms of partnered sexual activity, including penile–vaginal intercourse, anal sex and partnered masturbation.[5] When it comes to adolescent girls, the number of young women who reported neither solo nor partnered sexual behaviours increased during the same period. The boys are having less of it too, and while this is fairly shocking, I can't say that I'm surprised that teenagers in general are having less sex in this digital age. The rise of both social media and gaming has provided the kind of distraction that can become all-consuming.

So there are the facts and figures. But before we explore what the single women I spoke to about sex shared with me,

THRIVE SOLO

I would first like to address a theory of my own about why I personally seem to do OK without it.

Transmutation of Sex Desires

A few years ago, I read what is now one of my favourite books of all time: *Outwitting the Devil* by Napoleon Hill.[6] It is my belief that if you can master this classic self-help book, then you can master your life. Written back in 1938, the book wasn't initially published because Hill's wife was so worried about the negative backlash it was sure to provoke, due to its controversial take on the education system, the Church, and more. And so the book lay dormant until long after the author himself died in 1970, and was finally published in 2011.

Written as a metaphorical conversation between Hill and the Devil, the book's main premise is that individuals have the power to shape their lives through their thoughts and actions. It is a profound exploration of the human condition and the sinister forces that prevent us from achieving happiness and success. The book posits seven principles 'through which human beings may force life to provide them with spiritual, mental and physical freedom', so-called 'definiteness of purpose' being one. In brief, this is the idea that we can make our life whatever we want to so long as we are definite in our aims and plans. (Stay with me!)

In Chapter 10, 'Self Discipline', Hill discusses self-mastery, and how failure at this is the most destructive form of 'indefiniteness'. Three appetites, he says, are mainly responsible for a lack of self-discipline: the desire to eat, the desire to have sex, and the desire to express opinions. The Devil explains to Hill that when it comes to sex, one can master it 'by the simple process of transmuting that emotion into some form of activity other than copulation'. According to Hill, if we can learn to master and transmute the desire for sex, we can use it to our advantage by pouring that energy into other pursuits. In other words, sex energy is the most powerful, pure and creative energy there is, and when you're not using it to have actual sex, you can instead put it towards achieving all kinds of awesomeness.

Call me crazy, but as someone who *hasn't* been laid for more than four years, but who *has* thrown herself into several creative endeavours over the last few years, I'm loving this whole concept.

You may be wondering whether I'm clutching at straws here in order to justify a life without sex. Well, maybe. But maybe not. To clarify, what I'm *not* doing is inferring that we should all be intentionally giving up sex in order to pursue and fulfil our purpose in life; but what I *am* doing is suggesting that this notion isn't entirely ridiculous.

When I first read this chapter of *Outwitting the Devil*, it made complete sense to me – I would even describe it as a eureka moment. Because the truth is that I don't spend my time yearning for some bloke or fantasising about sex, because I'm far too busy throwing my energies into the things I'm passionate about – things that fulfil me and that I get a hell of a lot out of. My mind tends to be occupied with where my life is headed, or what I just learned from an inspiring podcast, or what trip I want to go on next, or coming up with ideas for work. In other words, by not clouding my mind with sex and everything that goes alongside it, I have far more time to spend on the things that are meaningful to me and, ultimately, make me happy. What's not to love?

I hasten to add that of course not every single woman who isn't sexually active feels so blasé about it, nor are they all necessarily in the throes of a passion project or some other endeavour. But I can't help but find Hill's ideas about transmuting our sex desires into the driving force for something

THRIVE SOLO

purposeful, meaningful or joyful to be both fascinating and somehow strangely validating. So I wanted to share them in case you might too.

Now it's time to find out what's going on in the minds of other single women. And let me start by saying that my research led me to the conclusion that there really is no one conclusion! There is no one way that single women experience sex, or lack thereof. Sex is a topic with much nuance and there are many variables at play. Being single doesn't necessarily mean that you're not having sex, or that you're having it; and if you're not having it, that doesn't necessarily mean that you are or aren't missing it. So let's consider the main themes that came up during my conversations with childfree, single women.

A Life without Sex: Positive, Negative . . . or Neutral?

I'm not sure what I was expecting when talking to single women about sex, but my conversations revealed that a considerable number of those who aren't getting it simply don't miss it. Maybe it's that 'out of sight, out of mind' thing I mentioned earlier; maybe in some cases it's an age thing; or maybe the need for it diminishes the longer you go without it. But whatever the reason, not everyone who is sexually inactive misses being sexually active. And interestingly, perhaps fewer people miss it than we might think . . .

This book is primarily a celebration of being single and, although *not* having sex isn't necessarily something to celebrate, it's interesting to consider that it certainly isn't always the loss that so many people assume it to be. In fact, oftentimes not having sex seems to be more . . . neutral.

The inimitable writer, storyteller and influencer Heidi Clements reflected this when she told me about her own feelings around sex:

Sex

❝ It's so funny because I have, I think, surprised myself by how I just don't think about it; and as someone who did enjoy sex while I was having it, it has surprised me how little I give a shit about it. I think there are so many myths about sex and sexuality and what you need as a human. And I've had so many people tell me that it's not normal to not have sex. And I'm like, I don't know. Is it? Maybe I'm lying to myself; maybe I'm going to get a boyfriend and it's just gonna be the greatest thing that ever happened to me, and I'm just gonna fuck all day long for seven years. I don't know. But as far as I do know, I'm fine! ❞

Heidi's neutrality towards sex was echoed by many of the women I spoke with, so let's delve deeper into some of the reasons why so many of us seem to do just fine without it.

We're Busy with Other Things

Karen (51, London) says that her reasons are very much aligned with Napoleon Hill's theory:

❝ I've actually surprised myself with how little sex even crosses my mind on a day-to-day basis. Yes, I might think about it occasionally, but more often than not, it's a fleeting thought rather than some kind of deep longing. I find that I'm so busy in my life, and there are so many things that take up my focus and my mental bandwidth – passion projects and things I'm working on – that it just isn't something that I'm preoccupied with. I'm sure that if I was to get into another relationship then that would change, but while I'm single, I seem to be totally unperturbed about not getting laid! ❞

THRIVE SOLO

Drea (38, North East England) is another who tends to throw her energies into other things. During our conversation about sex, she told me that like both Karen and me, 'when I'm in a relationship, I'm really into it. But when I'm not, I don't really care.' She went on to share this:

    ❝ Sex isn't something I'm searching out – maybe it's because my life is fulfilled in other ways, so I just don't have the time. But I'm sure if I was in a relationship, I'd be into it because I always have been before. But thinking about it now, I don't have the energy to seek it out. I can't be bothered. It's too much effort! Having to contend with other people's feelings and all of that? Do I have time for that? There's nothing in my brain that's saying, 'go find, go find, go find', and I wonder if that's because I don't have that sort of 'go and breed' mentality. ❞

So, ladies, if you're currently struggling with a lack of sex in your life, now might be the perfect time to keep busy by starting to work towards that dream of yours, whether this is in the form of an artistic outlet, a scientific research project or a long-abandoned hobby. Whatever it looks like for you, you'll be killing two birds with one stone.

Lack of Sex Drive

Of course one of the reasons for being happy living a life without sex is a lack of sex drive, and this is something that came up with several of the women I spoke to. For some, such as Drishti (33, Mumbai) and Rachel (36, Scotland), this is nothing new. Drishti told me that despite having had some good sex in her life, she has always had a relatively low sex drive, and her take-it-or-leave it attitude has caused issues in past relationships.

140

Sex

For Rachel, too, sex has never been a big thing, and her lack of drive has also proved to be an issue with previous partners. She explained further:

❝ In previous relationships, it was sometimes a cause of strain, because my male partner wanted more of a sex life, and I was kind of like, 'Well, it's not really something that's hugely important to me.' So I've been dating in the past four years, but I've got to the point now where I don't feel like it's making me feel any better. And it's not always great for your self-esteem. And so I've got to the stage where sex isn't something I miss an awful lot, you know? [. . .] I think there are other options as well when you're single – you can help yourself out sometimes as well! But yeah, it's not something that drives me, this needing to meet a man to have a shag. ❞

Some research shows that there really is a difference in the sex drives of men and women, with men's libido tending to be significantly stronger. One such study in 2001 reported that across many different studies, men show a higher frequency, and intensity, of sexual desire than women – reflected in more thoughts about sex, more sexual fantasies, a desire for more frequent intercourse, as well as a desire for a higher number of sexual partners.[7] Of course, men's libido is only a consideration for a woman if she is in a heterosexual relationship, and what's more, the issue of sex drive is highly nuanced and the data only really tells us about trends rather than how individual men and women compare,[8] so it should be taken with a pinch of salt. For example, a 2010 review of several studies revealed that up to nearly 20 per cent of men divulged that they had a significant lack of sexual desire – enough to be deemed problematic.[9]

There may be something else at play, too, at least for women of a certain age: menopause. (I will only touch on this very

THRIVE SOLO

briefly as I am not qualified to write about health issues in any detail.) Although sexual desire decreases for most (not all) men and women with age, women are far more likely to be affected by this decline in their sex drive. One study, 'Sexuality and Menopause', found that a majority of women 'experience some change in sexual function during the years immediately before and after menopause' with common problems including 'loss of desire, decreased frequency of sexual activity, painful intercourse'.[10] A more recent 2023 article in *Medical News Today* states that after menopause, women may experience any or all of low libido, fewer sexual thoughts and sexual fantasies, as well as physical changes that may impact their enjoyment of sex.[11] With regard to low libido, contributing factors can include hormonal changes, physical changes, and sociopsychological factors.

With all of this in mind, perhaps my own feelings of indifference around sex are impacted by several variables including being female, the menopause (which I'm very much in), and transmutation of my sex desires. But whether you're of a certain age, you don't have the desire for it, or you're too busy throwing your energies into a passion project, a lack of desire for sex seems to be one of the reasons why some of us are doing just fine without it.

You've Never Had Sex . . . or the Sex You've Had Wasn't All That

There are two other reasons I unearthed during my research as to why some long-term single women don't miss sex: they never really had it in the first place, or the sex they *did* have wasn't all that.

Gina (55, Los Angeles), a lifelong singleton, is someone for whom sex has never really been a part of life. Aside from one

Sex

year-long relationship, Gina has only had sex with a couple of people in her lifetime. She explained to me that she was someone who didn't have boyfriends while she was growing up, though she did eventually have sex with a couple of people while at college. Then, in her early forties, she met someone she was overwhelmingly attracted to, but the relationship only lasted a year and was more of a sexy, fun fling than anything serious.

When it comes to whether or not Gina misses sex now, here's what she had to say:

ff I'm a person who doesn't miss it because it was really only [something I experienced during] that one year of my life. And the things in my twenties were just sort of experiences – some good, mostly bad. So I think in a way, I am different from the people I know who've had long-term relationships – they have a different relationship to sex than I do. I feel like if you're missing it, it's because you had a lot of it, and it became a part of your life. So for me, it never became a part of my life. JJ

Maddie (50, Bristol) has similar views. She told me:

ff I don't miss it. I don't crave it. I don't really have much of a sex drive and I absolutely would not have a one-night stand in a million years, because I know myself, and I tend to become attached. Also, god, vibrators are so good now. And, quite honestly, I had a lot of really crap sex! I mean, god bless their hearts, I don't think any of them were very good at it. Whenever I was with a bloke, I'd have to kind of tell them what to do, like, 'Don't, no, stop doing that, because now you're just making me angry because now it just hurts.' I was like, 'What the fuck are you doing down there?!' JJ

143

THRIVE SOLO

Kailee (30, Jacksonville, North Carolina), meanwhile, has never had sex, and said that wanting it simply isn't part of her make-up:

> ❝ I identify as being on the spectrum of asexuality, and I've known it since I was very young. I'm actually heterosexual aromantic, meaning I can still have an emotional attachment to someone; I just don't have the desire to have a physical relationship. It's not important to me. That's not what I find value in. I want an emotional connection with someone, a spiritual connection. And some people don't really want to wait around for that. And I understand it, but I also don't think we should have to compromise who we are – that would be such a drain on your joy and your identity, and being asexual is just one small part of who I am. I have so many sources of value and meaning in my life – that's just one tiny facet. ❞

So it seems that for a surprisingly high number of women, sex is a somewhat neutral topic, sparking neither joy nor sorrow, and is not something they've participated much in, if at all, in the past.

Missing Sex and Intimacy

Although this book is primarily a celebration of being single and childfree, it's also important to acknowledge some of those aspects of a solo life that aren't so positive – and not having sex is certainly one of them for some single women.

Lindsey (45, West Sussex) is a case in point. Although she has had sex in various shorter relationships, what she craves is a deep connection and the kind of sex that would come from that:

144

Sex

❝ I really wanted to really go deep with sex with somebody, and that would take time because I'd want to get to know them and trust them. I am a bit upset and gutted that I've not managed to do that. I've just turned 45, and I feel a bit embarrassed about that sometimes – that I'm not massively sexually experienced. For me to be really sexually experienced, and to really discover my sexuality, I'd have to really trust somebody. [. . .] I do sometimes miss sex. I miss connection and touch because I have a deep desire to experience romantic love. When I watch programmes on TV where there's loads of sex, I hate having the negative emotions, but I'm human. I get really envious and I'm like, for fuck's sake! I'm pretty gutted that I can't have some sexual intimacy with a really nice man. But unfortunately at the moment it's just not available, and it hasn't been for quite some time. ❞

On the topic of sex on TV – which, as I mentioned, is the one thing that reawakens my own desires – this can also stir up some feelings in Pip (39, Isle of Wight). 'It's always so wonderful, isn't it, whatever you're watching?' she told me. 'Oh, it's all perfect, or it's romantic, or it's something like that! So yeah, that's what can spark something in me. You just think, oh god, that is so lovely.' Pip was also very candid with me about her other thoughts around missing sex:

❝ It is something that I definitely miss. I've actively tried to find somebody that I could have sex with and not be in a relationship with. But it's actually incredibly difficult! I've literally looked through Facebook friends and thought, 'Is he single?' And I've thought, 'Is there anybody who would fit into that category?' but I haven't come up with anybody. I used to go on dating apps, but

THRIVE SOLO

I wouldn't go on them now. It's the same as if you're looking for a relationship – it's just useless! It's just a massive waste of time. **"**

But Pip added that although she does miss sex, 'I certainly don't think about it on a daily basis. Not at all. I just seem to get periods of the month where I'll start looking at men. I feel like I wanna go out, and I want to show off, or I want to prowl about in front of them! I don't know if it's a hormonal thing.'

One woman who has a lot to say about her relationship with sex is Cerian (39, Dijon, Spain), who has been single for three and a half years since the end of her marriage. For the first 10 months after the split, Cerian wasn't interested in dating, but she subsequently went on to dating apps, 'which I'd never done before because they didn't exist when I was last single, and I went absolutely wild! At first it was fun, but I also realised it was making me extremely anxious.' Cerian went on to tell me that she struggles without regular sex, and that she thinks about it every day. 'I don't know if it's a lot every day, but I would say it's definitely every day.' Here's what else she had to say:

" In general, the sex thing is the most difficult thing. There's this idea that when you're single, you can just get on an app and go and have casual sex – which I have done quite a lot. But it's getting more and more difficult now because I don't want to do that any more. I don't want to just have sex with some random guy who's probably just not going to be very good. And I've also realised that since I gave up drinking two years ago, I definitely can't just have sex with anyone like I used to before. So that adds another layer of difficulty because then it's like, OK, if I want to have sex, I need to get to know someone a bit better. But then that's not really a casual situation. So, I do find it quite difficult, going

Sex

for long periods without it. But that's something I'm trying to get used to. **"**

But it's not just sex that Cerian misses; it's intimacy, too. And she's not alone. When she went on to tell me that 'I'm trying to get used to that need for physical affection', I asked Cerian whether she thought it was more about the physical affection or the sex. She told me that 'I sometimes think it might be more to do with the physical affection. Intimacy. People will say, well, just hug your friends. And that's nice, but sometimes you want a different kind of intimacy that you only get in a relationship, but doesn't necessarily mean it has to be sex.'

Maddie (50, Bristol) also confessed to missing intimacy even though she doesn't miss sex, saying that she 'was always more interested in affection. I think physical affection is lovely and there's times when I miss that'. And Kate (55, London), shared this:

" What I really miss is intimacy and sensuality. And that also can encompass sex, but for me it's a much wider palette of an experience that I miss. It's that animal connection and comfort. I'm quite a sensation junkie and I felt that intensely during the pandemic. You know when you see animals snuggled up together, there's a reason they're doing that, and we are animals, and I felt like I needed that. That's the bit that isn't always organised in my life that I would like more, and that I do miss. I hanker after intimacy and sensuality with another person; but I'm also willing to wait for something that feels good. It's not the end of my world if it doesn't come along. But I'm very much open to seeing what might come along. **"**

THRIVE SOLO

So, there's no denying that one of the downsides for *some* single women is the enforced celibacy that they are experiencing. But it's not all doom and gloom – there are some women for whom being single provides a distinct advantage when it comes to sex.

I'll Have What She's Having

For some, not being stuck within the confines of a traditional relationship means we can explore and experience sex in a refreshingly different way. Intrigued? Let's explore . . .

Sex outside of the Traditional Relationship

Marianne Power is someone who knows all about this. In her book, *Love Me! One Woman's Search For a Different Happy Ever After*, she explores how, as a 40-something woman, you can still have a life with love and sex and family if you *don't* go down the road of partnership and kids.[12] Marianne, by her own admission, was always insecure about sex, not least because of her upbringing as an Irish-Catholic convent schoolgirl and 'not the fun, naughty kind, but the really repressed kind'. She told me that, for many years, she believed that everyone else knew what they were doing, whereas she didn't. She also wondered why she didn't seem to want a 'normal' partnership, even though she thought sex was important.

A few years ago, Marianne was given the opportunity to attend a tantra retreat. This started off as her ultimate nightmare – a group of strangers talking openly about sex and practising various things on each other – and she almost didn't go; but by the end it was so transformational that she attended a second retreat. Marianne told me that the retreats were incredibly healing for her and her relationship with sex, and that she was 'so, so glad I faced up to my shame and insecurities round sex', ultimately resolving them. She has subsequently built a life that consists of several 'beautiful lovers' and she told me that she is now exactly where she wants to be and that she has a lot of love and friendship and sex in her life. 'I have friends and lovers – that's how I would describe it. I've managed to find this way where I have deep connections, and also my freedom, which I always seem to really want. I always felt constricted when I was in more official relationships. It just didn't suit me.'

She explains further:

" Maybe for some people sex isn't a very important part of life; we all have different desires and different things that are important to us. For me, I always had the sense that it was [important], and I feel quite myself when I'm with someone in that way. I'm really glad to be in this place now where I can enjoy sex and enjoy love, and not necessarily in the traditional dynamics of relationships and 'now we're boyfriend and girlfriend, and now we'll probably move in in a year' – they call it the relationship escalator, when you get on and there's this path. That never worked for me. So I find the way that I can have sex and closeness – you know, they're really close relationships, they're not casual, they're not throw-away one-night stands – but they're not coming within that traditional boyfriend-girlfriend container. "

While Kristi (38, Estherville) doesn't have multiple lovers, when she's 'on the prowl', she has a friends-with-benefits arrangement with a male friend she's known for 10 years. Kristi refers to him as her 'maintenance man' and I was intrigued to find out more. She told me:

THRIVE SOLO

❝ This one guy and I have been friends for a good 10 years. He's like the male version of me, and I'm like the female version of him. And we just get together when we need it, and leave each other alone when we're good. And it's not very often – he's on the road a lot. So yeah, when we think we need some time, we just get together and have some time, and then we go on our way. I just deal with it when I get the urge. ❞

And, finally, Julie (43, Walla Walla, Washington) told me that for her it's about 'meeting people when you travel and just seeing what happens. Friends with benefits or casual relationships. Some like dating just for fun. There are many less-discussed and less marital-driven ways to incorporate sexual and romantic pleasure into our lives without giving up the benefits of our solo life.'

So there you have it. A friends-with-benefits set-up, multiple situationships with a variety of partners, and other situations besides can be a wonderful way of incorporating sex into your life. But let's not forget that there is, of course, a way that we haven't touched on yet . . .

Self-Love, Baby

There is another way of partaking in sexual activity that involves nobody but yourself. And despite the fact that the vast majority of us have done it in our lives, it remains a somewhat taboo subject.

For my own part, masturbation was something I discovered relatively early on in life, although I'm not willing to go *so* far outside my comfort zone as to admit exactly when 'early' was. Spoilsport, I know. Outside of relationships (and, let's be honest, inside relationships too) it was definitely a regular occurrence in my life, not least because it was a guaranteed way of reaching orgasm. (Am I alone when I say that it's often a far quicker and easier way of climaxing than with a partner? Am I?!) I digress . . .

According to a comprehensive survey of the sex lives of Americans in 2010, more than half of women aged 18 to 49 said that they'd masturbated alone in the previous 90 days, regardless of whether they were in a relationship or not.[13] In addition, AgriTech company Univia reported that 96 per cent of the people they spoke to masturbate at least once a month.[14] So, with that, let's drop the shame and look at some of the benefits of pleasuring oneself. Research suggests that sexual stimulation through masturbation can reduce stress, make us sleep better, boost concentration, alleviate pain and, erm, improve sex.[15] Glossing over that last one, there are a host of health benefits available to us when we get jiggy with ourselves. As if that wasn't enough, having an orgasm increases the blood flow throughout our bodies, releasing those feel-good endorphins that we're all after. Gloria Brame, PhD, said that an 'orgasm is the biggest non-drug blast of dopamine available'.[16] In other words, having an orgasm through masturbation creates feelings of euphoria. And back to my previous point, sometimes us ladies are far more adept at bringing ourselves to climax, but if not, we can always turn to a sex toy to help us along . . .

Lindsey, whose life coach is 'absolutely obsessed by self-pleasure', talked her into buying a yoni wand, a phallic object made from crystals and designed as a natural alternative to plastic sex toys. While Lindsey has 'always self-pleasured', she shared that it had always been pretty limiting, but went on to say: 'I know that there's a whole world to investigate that will allow me to give myself phenomenal orgasmic experiences.' And while we're on the subject of sex toys, *The State of Self-Love & Masturbation* report of 2023 revealed that 63 per cent of respondents consider the act of sexual self-love to be a critical part of their self-care routine.[17] *Who knew?!* And if toys are your

THRIVE SOLO

thing, never has it been easier to acquire as many as you like, without the need to skulk shamefully into a Soho sex shop to browse the shelves while inwardly praying you don't bump into your old schoolteacher (although who that would be more embarrassing for is debatable).

The rise of online shopping has made it so much easier for us coy Brits to satisfy our sex toy needs, despite potentially having to deal with a knowing smirk from the Amazon delivery guy. Interestingly, research published by Statista Research Department shows that sex toys are very much on the rise, and the global sex toy market is expected to grow from $27.17 billion in 2019, to $80.7 billion by 2030.[18]

I'll finish this section off with some eloquent and insightful words from Julie (43, Walla Walla, Washington):

> ❝ I think that there is so much more to pleasure and sexuality than just intercourse or whatever you choose. There is sensuality in nature, in food, in our curated home environment. I believe as solo individuals, we must be intentional about maintaining a certain amount of physical touch and pleasure in our lives for our own physiological health. This does not have to equal dating, hook-ups or marriage. It can be whatever interests you or that you are comfortable with. It can be curating a beautiful sensual environment. The way you take care of your body. Masturbation of your choice. ❞

If this section has had your toes curling for all the wrong reasons, maybe now is the time to consider embracing some sexy self-love – sex toys optional – and join the other 63 per cent of people who consider it essential to their well-being. You'll never know unless you give it a try.

Final Thoughts

There is no one way that single women experience sex. From those who yearn for it, to those who rarely think about it, to those who are having it with multiple people, sex – and our emotions around it – vary as much as all the wonderful single women themselves. And whatever it looks and feels like for you, whether good or bad, your experience is valid.

If you're one of those women who isn't currently having sex, and you miss the intimacy that goes with it, please know that you are not alone. Hopefully this chapter might have inspired you to explore an avenue you haven't been down before. And if you're not currently channelling all of your sex energy into some weird and wonderful life project, you can console yourself that, at the very least, you're not having any *bad* sex. I'll take a little 'self-love' over that any day.

—Podcast Pearls—

'My life doesn't need a romantic partner to legitimise it, or complete it. But if that happens, that person really does have to be adding to the life that I've found for myself and created for myself, and that I nurture. They would really have to be making that better because I'm not willing to risk what I have for somebody who isn't that person.'

— Amy Key (46, London)

8

FRIENDSHIPS AND OTHER RELATIONSHIPS

'My friends are the most important aspect of my single life.'
— PIP (39, ISLE OF WIGHT)

Something seldom spoken about when it comes to us single, childfree women are the many other non-romantic relationships that we have in our lives, the time we have to nurture these, and how they often provide much of the emotional support that any human requires.

This aspect of singledom tends to get lost in a narrative that focuses purely on what single women 'lack', rather than what can be gained from the other people in their lives. Yes, a romantic partner and our own children are not present, but for that exact reason we can often benefit from space in our life for an abundance of friends and other relationships. In many cases, it's precisely because we're free in ways that married mothers are not that these 'other' relationships can have space to flourish.

As single, childfree women we are in the incredibly fortunate position of having an abundance of both time and energy

THRIVE SOLO

to invest in being a very present daughter, friend, sister, aunt, neighbour, teacher . . . the list goes on! There is so much to be gained from other relationships, but as a society we tend to be distracted by placing the vast majority of emphasis on romantic relationships, consequently overlooking the other, equally important, connections in all of our lives.

In this chapter, we'll focus on how not being in a relationship and not having kids can impact our friendships and other relationships in a positive manner.

Friendship

In Aristotle's *The Nicomachean Ethics*, he writes: 'friendship is among the most indispensable requirements of life: it is, in fact, a necessary means to life.'[1] So, according to Aristotle (who apparently was pretty smart), friendship is a vitally important part of life, yet we do not put it on a pedestal in the same way we do romantic relationships. Why is this?

While our culture continues to prioritise romantic relationships, there is more and more research to show the importance of friendships in terms of our well-being and longevity. For example, a 2020 study in *The American Journal of Psychiatry* found that those people who have close friends are more satisfied with their lives and are also less likely to suffer from depression.[2] And a 2023 study found that although we can reap the benefits of friendship from other sources, it was clear that friendship is 'a special type of relationship' that makes a unique contribution to our well-being, and friendships that last through the years are considered to be vital for us to flourish psychologically.[3] Essentially, high-quality adult friendships are significant predictors of well-being and can even protect us against mental health issues such as anxiety and depression.

Friendships and Other Relationships

This is all great news for single, childfree people who have more time to invest in friendships.

Lindsey (45, West Sussex) talked about how being single and not having kids means 'having the energy to put into cultivating friendships, because I'm not putting that energy into a relationship. Because relationships do need energy, and they deserve energy, and they are work, aren't they? So for me, I think it has enabled me to always be there for my friends.' Jenna (37, Brighton) added that being single means appreciating her friendships more, and that 'we put more effort into them because they're more of a priority – when you're in a relationship, friends can become an afterthought.' Jenna explained how she moved from London to Brighton and could put the effort into finding herself a group of great friends who are 'always around for each other. It's worked out really nicely, but like I say, none of this would've happened if it weren't for being single.'

Christine (53, Atlanta, Georgia) echoed these sentiments, saying that being single 'just gives me more time to cultivate friendships. For example, I stay in touch with quite a few of my former students; and I have colleagues who are married, and they definitely do not keep in touch with their students anywhere near as much as I do. I think being single affords you so much more time to devote to your relationships. Just that alone has had a significant effect.' Laura (49, Surrey) reiterated this idea when she told me this:

> ❝ This is not to criticise people who are married with kids, because I know lots of people who are married with kids who've got loads of friends and are amazing friends. But I think when you're single and childfree, you just have more time to invest in, and nurture, friendships. You aren't spreading yourself across friends, and a husband, and children, which

THRIVE SOLO

automatically means that you're spreading yourself thinner. Also, I feel that you've got more time to be their emotional support. For example, I have a friend who recently lost her partner. I was able to drop everything and literally move into her flat at really short notice, so that she wasn't on her own, and spend three days with her. Had I been married with kids, it would've been very hard for me to do that. You can really be there for other people. **"**

Friends as Family and Significant Others

While most of us understand and appreciate the significance of close friendships in our lives – and indeed, it's often our friends we turn to when our romantic relationship is in trouble – the idea of friendship as 'the' central relationship is still an alien concept that doesn't carry quite the same weight. No matter how close a friendship one might have, when push comes to shove, it's our romantic relationships that take precedence over and above everyone and everything else. Strange when you think about it.

If, like me, you're a (slightly obsessed) fan of the TV show *Grey's Anatomy*, you'll be familiar with the close friendship between Meredith Grey and Christina Yang, whose various romantic interests are given a run for their money by the bond that these two women share. Referring to each other as their 'person', it's genuinely heartwarming to watch Meredith and Christina's friendship portrayed as the most important relationship in both of their lives, or at the very least, equal to their relationships with their partners.

One of my previous podcast guests, Rebecca Traister, writes about this concept of having a friend as your 'person' in her book, *All The Single Ladies*.[4] Rebecca believes firmly that we have

Friendships and Other Relationships

to get better at speaking more openly about the importance of our friendships and the roles they have in our lives. She thinks that even though friendships are not formalised in our lives (in the same way that a romantic partnership is often formalised through a wedding), we need to speak up about them.

It was, ironically, in the run-up to her own marriage that Rebecca had the idea to write a book about single women. The general reaction to the news of her engagement shocked Rebecca, who had already been living, as she told me, 'a complete, full adult life' for many years. However, 'the thing that I experienced at that point [on announcing her engagement] was the treatment of society, including friends and family, treating me at 35, as though my adult life were just beginning. And this was horrifying to me. This was chilling to me.'

As someone who considers her best friends as extensions of her family, Rebecca's take on this resonated with me deeply, and it's encouraging to hear a married woman acknowledge this issue in such a way.

Speaking to other women about their friendships, it was immediately obvious that many viewed them with the same importance as Rebecca and I do. As Lindsey (45, West Sussex) told me:

> ❝ We as a society don't put friendship, or talk about friendship, as being important. It's always romantic love and family. But for some people, friendships are the ultimate important relationship in their lives. They are our family. Friendships have always been the most important relationships in my whole life, and I think always will be. My friends know me more than anybody. ❞

And, of course, the thing about friendships that sets them apart from familial relationships, is that you actually get to choose them. Laura (49, Surrey) says her friends are her 'world' and she enjoys investing a lot of time and energy in them

THRIVE SOLO

because she views them as chosen family. In fact, Laura thinks you develop even stronger bonds with friends than you do with family. Christine (53, Atlanta, Georgia) agrees wholeheartedly with this, especially as someone who isn't close to her blood family. She even chooses to spend Christmas and Thanksgiving with her chosen family rather than her actual family.

Karen (51, London), who also isn't close to her own family, told me how vital her friends are to her. She explains:

> ❝ I'm very happily single and childfree, but that doesn't mean I don't rely heavily on my friends who, by the way, might as well be my blood relatives. My closest girlfriends provide me with a real sense of security and belonging, because I know for absolute certain that they are always there for me, no matter what. When you're a solo woman, it can feel hard sometimes not having that family unit of your own, so it's difficult to articulate how having a 'family of friends' changes the game. I'm an only child, and I'm not close to my parents, but I know that I will always have somewhere to spend Christmas, Easter, New Year's . . . you name it!
>
> Truly, I am so, so grateful for these women in my life who are my emotional, mental, physical and spiritual support system. And the best thing is that, unlike when you're married and it's just you and your partner, having several women in my life who are essentially family means that I get to lean on a different one, depending on a particular need. One in particular I would go to if I was feeling low, for example, whereas there's another who I would always go to if I needed help with something. It's wonderful. ❞

So for many of us singles, we really do consider our friends as family where we don't have a traditional family unit of our own. In some cases, this can be taken even further when a friendship becomes, to all intents and purposes, the equivalent of a romantic relationship.

On the more radical end of the spectrum of close friendships, author Rhaina Cohen explores the lives of people who have defied convention by choosing a friend as their life partner in her book, *The Other Significant Others*.[5] She tells the story of Kami West and Kate Tillotson, or Tilly, whose friendship is very much the central relationship in their lives. Kami had been dating a boyfriend for only a matter of weeks when she told him, in no uncertain terms, that he was – and always would be – outranked by her best friend. As Kami pointed out, Tilly was there before him, and would be there after him, and in the meantime, she would remain Kami's number-one priority. As a result, said boyfriend attempted to sabotage the friendship between the two women by calling Tilly 'a slut and a bad influence'. Funnily enough, that particular relationship ended at Kami's behest, and she subsequently vowed never to let another man put a strain on her friendship with Tilly.

As Rhaina told me in our interview, 'the world was not built for extremely deep friendships' yet 'friendship can be a bigger, deeper and more central relationship to our lives than we've been told.' She also told me about her own experience of a very significant friendship in which 'the two of us were trying to find language to talk about each other. Like "best friend" felt like it didn't actually cut it' and when it came to other people, 'we constantly had to explain what we were – it was confusing to feel like we were this species that no one had identified yet.' Rhaina wrote in a 2020 article for *The Atlantic* that many people who centralise a friendship rather than a romantic relationship find that their decision seems incomprehensible to other people; but as Rhaina also wrote, these significant friendships could actually be held up as models of how we might, as a society, 'expand our conceptions of intimacy and care'.[6]

These examples may seem a tad intense or even confusing to those of us who have not experienced this level of friendship before, but they do demonstrate the opportunities that our friendships can provide in terms of happiness, fulfilment and deep connection. And it's an interesting contrast to the romantic-relationship-obsessed narrative we normally see.

Varied Friendships

One of the things I found most interesting when speaking to single women about friendship was how being single seems to lend itself to having more variety in the kinds of relationships we cultivate. That isn't to say that our coupled counterparts don't also have a variety of different friends, but perhaps when you're married with kids, there's more of a tendency to hang out with other married mums, as opposed to the 25-year-old bloke you met at a gig last year, or the 76-year-old neighbour you regularly share a bottle of wine with, who often has you howling with laughter as she regales stories from her misspent youth. And as they say: variety is the spice of life!

Whereas a life of marriage and children tends to mean many friends of similar age and circumstances, being single allows for a veritable hotchpotch of different relationships, not least because we're better suited to being more intentional about who we hang out with and have more time to widen our friendship circle as well as maintain friendships with people in different countries. For the majority of my married friends with kids, their circle consists largely of other married mothers whom they have met through NCT groups or at the school gates; and while there is of course nothing wrong with this, it's possibly more limiting than the friendship opportunities you're afforded when you're living a solo life.

Maddie (50, Bristol) talked about how being single means that while she doesn't have 'that one person who knows me

Friendships and Other Relationships

inside out', she has a variety of different people who are there for her 'at different moments, for different reasons'. Although she isn't able to look to one particular person for consistent support, what she gains instead is the same level of consistency and support and love from many different people, in different ways and at different times. What Maddie gains from her variety of relationships is not only people who are 'quite alternative' but also 'the different energy' that she gets from each of them, which speaks 'to different aspects of me'. Maddie also told me that she believes her friendship circle is wider, more varied and more interesting because she's put herself out there more due to her single status, pursuing hobbies and interests with the intention of making new friends. She pointed out that when we're in a relationship, we have a tendency to turn inwards rather than looking out into the world for new people and friendships. I can relate to this myself, having done exactly this in many of my previous relationships.

Pip (39, Isle of Wight) also talked about how much she gains from having a variety of friends in her life, thanks to her single status. 'It's been like creating a patchwork soulmate from different areas of my life,' she said, and explained how not following the traditional path in life has opened her mind and meant that she's always been drawn to a wide variety of people who tend to 'fit outside the box'. In her view, being single and childfree makes for many more interesting interactions in life. I concur.

Laura (49, Surrey) told me that being single means she has 'more time and headspace to be more discerning about friendships,' and that she has a more diverse group of friends compared to her married friends with kids because a lot of them didn't really choose their friends. Laura explains that her married friends tend to have friendships of convenience – ones forged by necessity because they have kids who are the same age and are doing similar things. What's more, because

THRIVE SOLO

everything revolves around the children, her friends don't have time to go out and explore friendships with people they might actually want to be friends with.

Laura subsequently feels that she has a more diverse friendship group in terms of where she met her friends, how she met them, their ages and their backgrounds.

It's interesting that Laura mentioned that she has friends of different ages because intergenerational friendships came up several times with many of the women I spoke to, and are something they attributed to their single status. There could be a number of reasons for this, including our schedules allowing us more time for people outside of our immediate peer group, less need for validation and support from other people in the same scenario (e.g. other mums), and perhaps also a certain open-mindedness that being single lends itself to because we're swimming against the tide of the traditional life path.

Gráinne (41, Ireland) told me about one such friendship, which came about when she lived in Scotland and would meet up every Sunday with Rita, who is 103 years old. Even though Gráinne no longer lives locally, they are still in touch by letter and Gráinne visits Rita whenever she is in Scotland. Gráinne also organises community tea events for other women in their seventies, eighties and beyond and has a lot of fun chatting to the ladies who attend. When reflecting on why she enjoys this so much, Gráinne said: 'They've just done so much. I love, love, love hanging out with people my own age too, but I find older people just so fascinating, and so funny.'

When I asked her if she thought she would have done these kinds of things had she got married and had kids, Gráinne simply said: 'No. I have so much more time to do this as I'm single.' She added that she has a wide network of friends because she's been able to throw herself into various groups. As she rightly says, it takes effort to build up these networks, and in her case,

Friendships and Other Relationships

not having a partner or parenting responsibilities has made many of these things possible for her.

A patchwork quilt of friendships can also show up in terms of geographical location. For example, Gráinne also has friends who are spread far and wide across the world. She uses her holiday allowance to visit them and has managed to keep up with friendships in multiple countries over decades.

Sinead (50, Dublin) is another whose friendship group includes lots of people who live in other countries – something she too attributes to not having kids and a husband, which has allowed her to travel solo to meet new people and visit friends.

So, as these stories attest, being single and childfree enables you to potentially have a wider range of friends, and to select them on their merit rather than convenience. And, young or old, near or far, being friends with people of different ages and backgrounds is enriching and can be life-affirming, as it helps us to see the world through an entirely different lens.

Losing Friends When They Become Parents

We can't talk about friendship in this context without acknowledging the loss that we often experience as our friends couple up and start families of their own. Before hearing from some women about what this has looked like in their own lives, let's have a look at some of the research around families.

Gathering their data from the National Survey of Families and Households (1992–1994) and the General Social Survey (2000, 2004, 2006, 2012), Sarkisian and Gerstel ascertained in their study that marriage tends to make people more insular, so we should stop promoting it over and above everything else.[7] Instead, there should be an acknowledgement that it's actually the single people among us who tend to be more involved with their broader communities.

THRIVE SOLO

In a 2012 research study, Kelly Musick and Larry Bumpass followed more than 2000 people for several years, beginning when they were aged under 50 and single.[8] Interestingly, but perhaps not surprisingly, the people who ended up living with a partner – whether married or not – became more insular. They also spent less time with both their parents and their friends than when they were single, and this was still the case six years down the line, rather than just as some temporary effect of the 'honeymoon period' that many of us are, no doubt, familiar with.

Michèle Barrett and Mary McIntosh also spoke to this some years earlier in their 1982 book *The Anti-Social Family,* which was described at the time as a 'very daring critique of the family'.[9] There is a section called 'Family Gains and Social Losses' in which they talk about the traditional family unit as having drawn 'comfort and security into itself and left the outside world bereft'. In other words, Barrett and McIntosh believe that it's not that the world has been a 'pre-existing harsh climate' that has forced family units to turn inwards, but rather that family units have turned inwards, and it is this that has made the world seem 'cold and friendless'. They add that the world would be a more caring and loving place if families didn't claim all of the caring and loving for themselves. This may sound like a rather harsh point, but I can kind of see where they're coming from.

This other side of friendship when you're single and child-free cropped up in almost every conversation I had regarding this topic. At best, your coupled friends with kids are no longer able to give so much to your friendship, and at worst you may lose them altogether to the whirlwind that is a partner and young children. Of course this is a completely natural part of life, and none of the women I spoke to expressed any resentment towards their friends with families of their own – it is, after all, understandable. But I would like to address the sadness and grief that can come from being a single, childless woman whose friends and peers have all journeyed down a very different path from you.

Friendships and Other Relationships

The gap between those women who have children and those who don't can manifest in a variety of different ways. Sometimes the distance is literal, and we don't physically see our friends with kids as much, but sometimes it's metaphorical, and when we *do* see them, they're distracted, or being constantly interrupted by one or more of their children.

Gráinne (41, Ireland), for example, said, 'I would say I'm actually more present with my friends when we're together, because my friends who have kids always have their kids on their minds, because they're good mums – but it can mean that they're not really listening or taking in what's going on in my life.' Laura told me about a recent trip that she took for a few days with a friend and her children, saying that 'I didn't have one conversation with her the whole time we were away.' Every time they tried to chat, one of the children would join in and 'she just let them interrupt'.

Another way that this gap or loss can manifest is in the amount of time and effort our friends are able to extend to us. Drea (38, North East England) said that she's always the one who has to make the effort because it's 'easier' for her. She adds, 'But my time is just as precious and important as their time, although sometimes it doesn't feel as valued – or as equal – because of my situation versus theirs.' Victoria (38, Harrogate) mentioned a sense of drifting away from an old friend with whom she travelled the world, since she had kids. Victoria lived in Malaysia for many years, and in the three years since she's been back in the UK, she's only seen her friend once. 'Every so often I'll get a text, but she never, ever asks me about my life.'

Lindsey, too, told me this about how children have affected some of her friendships:

> ❝ They haven't got the time, and they haven't got the energy. And it's been hard. I just miss them so much. And it's not that they've not got the inclination, because I know that if they could in this busy

modern-day world, they would be spending more time with me, and we'd be going off, and money wouldn't be an issue, and we'd go away for weekends and this, that, and the other. A lot of my friends are bringing up kids on their own as well. So the money's affected. They've not got the child support. There's loads of issues. But yeah, I really do miss my friends. And you just know that your friendship's going to change for the next 15, 20 years. 🍳

A final aspect of this theme is the way in which single, child-free women can be negatively perceived and treated by those with children, as a result of their different life circumstances. Christine (53, Atlanta, Georgia) told me that she has found that some friendships have really declined and gotten worse as it's become clearer and clearer over time that it's highly unlikely that she will marry, and she's definitely not going to have kids. She adds that in her experience, for many people, being friends with somebody who's single and childless is potentially an issue, unless they've known that person for a long time.

Christine added that some of those negative perceptions can come from family members – something that she's all too familiar with. In fact, her single, childfree status has profoundly impacted the relationship she has with several family members, and she divulged that she's barely on speaking terms with some of them. And while Lindsey *is* close to her family, her single, childless status has also to some extent affected the relationship she has with her family:

🍳 I think my family would've visited me more if I'd had kids. I think it would've brought the grandparents down to me, rather than me always being the one that's going up there. My family are working-class northern, and from a different generation. And I think even if I had a man, my dad would feel more comfortable

Friendships and Other Relationships

coming down – you know, couples with couples, and all that. Also, I think my sister would've possibly come down more because she would be an aunt – especially if I'd had a daughter, because she didn't have daughters, and she just loves little girls. Whereas now it's more me going up there. Also, no one's ever come to my house for Christmas dinner, and no one ever will come to my house for Christmas dinner, unless I get a partner and/or children. And it's fine. I get it. But it's silent bias, isn't it? Silent bias that they're not even aware of. 🙶

Despite Lindsey's experience, she has made peace with the situation, as has Laura, who very much leans into the new friends she's made along the way. She told me that she chooses to focus her energies on the new friendships she's cultivated and has now made peace with letting certain friendships go. As she rightly points out, friendships don't have to last forever, and nor should all of them – some friends are meant to come in and out of our lives, just as so many romantic relationships do. I can relate to both Laura and Lindsey, in that while I've experienced a certain amount of sadness and grief for the friends I've drifted apart from, I'm also incredibly grateful for the new friendships I've made *thanks* to my being single and not having kids.

Family

My sister has four children, three of whom are triplets, and then their older brother. Three are boys and one is a girl – my beloved niece, Blue. One of the greatest joys of my life has been my relationship with these four humans, all of whom I love to pieces. They used to think I was the coolest person on the planet; these days, not so much, but I suppose that's only to be expected given that they are now young adults. I've been lucky

THRIVE SOLO

enough to live only a 30-minute drive away from them, and so have always been very much involved in their lives due to the close relationship I have with my sister. And what a blessing it's been to have had the time to pour into them over the years, cultivating relationships with all four of them, and knowing that I've been a big part of their childhoods.

One of the most underrated benefits of being a single, childfree woman is the extra time we're afforded to nurture those relationships in our lives that might otherwise be somewhat neglected, my sister being a case in point. I've wondered on many occasions whether I would have been so close to her if I'd had kids of my own, and I think it's safe to say that no, I would not. While I'm also close to my brother, he lives abroad and until very recently didn't have children of his own.

When my first nephew was born, I spent a ridiculous amount of quality time with him, often having him for sleepovers, babysitting him and building the bond that remains to this day – albeit he's not quite as into me as he was when he was three, or seven or even 15! But there's a deep-rooted connection that I can't help thinking wouldn't have developed had I been busy with a family of my own. It was the same when the triplets came along. Playing a significant role in the lives of these children is something I will be forever grateful for, and my relationship with Blue in particular is more like that of sisters than auntie and niece. When I asked Blue if she thought we were closer because I haven't had children of my own, she replied, 'I think so, because you just wouldn't spend as much time with us. Also, probably the last thing you'd want to do is hang out with more teenagers.' Fair point.

One of the most precious things about being an auntie – especially a childfree one – is that you become a steady influence in the lives of your niblings (the children of one's siblings), which is something that shouldn't be underestimated. While

Friendships and Other Relationships

they may be having ups and downs with one or both parents, you can be the island of calm in the eye of the inevitable storms they will experience. And somehow the physical distance that is inherent in being an aunt can be a real advantage. You're always there in the background, a presence they know will have their backs, but who is never too close for comfort. There's an anonymous quote I love that says: 'Only an aunt can give hugs like a mother, can keep secrets like a sister and share love like a friend.' I think that sums up being an aunt for me pretty perfectly. However close or distant I may be with any one of them at any particular time, I know that *they* know I'm always there if and when they need me. And that, my friends, is magic.

Extra Time for Our Parents

Many of the women I spoke to about their relationships mentioned similar benefits to being single and childfree when it comes to the time they have to nurture connections with their parents. Take Maddie (50, Bristol), for example, who is particularly close to her mum. Maddie was close to both of her parents when she was growing up, and believes that the closeness and depth of both relationships might not have developed in the same way into adulthood had she married and had kids. Sadly, Maddie lost her dad 20 years ago, but she and her mum remain close, even more so since her dad passed.

Lindsey (45, West Sussex) told me that she was able to take her mum away for her 70th birthday: 'Just me and her, and it was just beautiful. Would I have done that if I'd had a child? Maybe not.' Lindsey also told me that she thought she had deeper conversations with her parents because she doesn't have children of her own to distract them all.

THRIVE SOLO

Laura (49, Surrey), who like Maddie has lost her dad, told me this about her relationship with her mum:

❝ When my dad died, I was able to literally put my life on hold for my mum because she was in such a bad way. And I actually felt really grateful at that point that I didn't have a partner and children, because if I'd tried to support her and also be a wife and mother, it would've destroyed me at the same time as grieving my dad. But because I didn't have that, I was able to completely focus on my mum. And she knew that if I'd had a husband and kids, I wouldn't have been able to stay with her more than a few days. I feel like my relationship with my mum is probably even stronger because I'm able to give a lot more emotional support, time and practical support. And that's something I'm really grateful for. ❞

This availability that comes from not having dependents in the form of a partner and children is especially beneficial when a parent is unwell. Nancy (60, Boulder, Colorado) – an author, life coach and previous podcast guest – told me this when I asked her what she thought the best thing is about being single and childfree:

❝ I could say a million things – waking up alone, having my own time, blah, blah, blah – but really from this moment right here, I'm at my parents' house. My father's in the hospital. He's OK. I've been here now for a month. Last year my mother was diagnosed with brain cancer and had a mastectomy. I was here for six weeks. That's for me the best thing about being single. My sister is married – she's been able to be here back and forth both times – but she has a husband, and a dog, and two kids. She has a family that she needs to go to. The blessing right now of being single in my life is getting to spend this unexpected time with my parents as an adult, late in their lives and at a time in my life that I wouldn't ever have expected to get this bonus time with them. That, right now, is the best blessing of being single. 🥂

So, when it comes to our families, and particularly our parents for those of us lucky enough to still have them, being single can truly be a gift.

Final Thoughts

As we've heard from the various voices in this chapter, there is so much goodness to be found in the friendships made outside of the conventional life path. We have more time to cultivate and nurture friendships, more freedom to find new friends, a more open mind *and* a more open calendar. We tend to cultivate a diversity of friendships, rather than sticking to the ones that are made out of convenience and/or the shared experience of motherhood. And as Lindsey (45, West Sussex) pointed out, it's great to have friends without kids because 'there's so much fun to be had in the world as adults playing and experiencing joy.' As single women, we can be intentional about our friends, taking the time to invest in those people who light us up no matter their age, background or relationship status. And we can also take care of the people in our lives who really need us, in a way that might not be possible if we had a family of our own to look after. Sounds like a pretty good deal to me.

THRIVE SOLO

—Podcast Pearls—

'[Being single and childfree has] allowed me to do some travelling, and to be a bit more spontaneous in life, and to be there for others as well; I've got lots of friends with children who are in relationships, and who really need a single, childfree friend there for support sometimes. That sense of being able to be there for a range of different people is just fantastic.'

— Jayne (45, Bristol)

CONCLUDING THOUGHTS

and Eight Practical Tips

'I'm becoming the person that I'm supposed to be. There is this strong, authentic, creative, cool woman in there who has had the space to grow.'

— MADDIE (50, BRISTOL)

We've come to the final chapter, and I sincerely hope that you're beginning to believe it's more than possible to thrive solo – or, at the very least, you're beginning to realise that a single, childfree life can be just as fabulous as a conventional one. Perhaps you're already feeling pretty happy, in which case, I hope that this exploration has simply validated your thoughts and feelings or given you even more to feel grateful for in your single life. I'm even hoping that some of you might have had your minds opened to the possibility that, in some ways, a solo life can afford you many freedoms, gifts and opportunities that aren't so easily accessible when you have a partner and children.

But it goes without saying that whichever path life takes you down is guaranteed to present you with both joys and sorrows, regardless of whether you're married with kids or single without them. Because, as far as I'm concerned, it's more to do with how you feel within yourself, and about yourself, than it is to do with your external circumstances. We are all individual, autonomous human beings whose worth should never be measured by either a partner or by children. And a

THRIVE SOLO

truth of life, at least one that I believe, is that it's all an inside job. Each and every one of us should be cultivating our own sense of self-worth and internal peace that isn't reliant upon anyone else's presence or absence.

How to Do the Inner Work

At the time of writing, I'm 48 years old and have been single for almost seven years. It wouldn't be beyond the realms of possibility for somebody to presume that, being single and childless, I might not be particularly joyful or particularly fulfilled. But the funny thing is that I'm more joyful and more fulfilled than I ever have been at any other stage in my life. I am all the proof you need that if it's possible for me, then it's possible for anyone to be feeling bloody great.

In many ways, I believe it's *because* I'm single and childless that I feel so good. The fulfilment part of the equation is largely because, several years ago, I decided to take control of my life, and, perhaps even more importantly, take responsibility for it. I have a plan, and I have goals that I work towards little by little each day. None of those goals has anything to do with a partner or children – they have to do with myself, my life and where I'm headed. The joy part of the equation is because I've finally realised that joy is something that any one of us can find and cultivate all by ourselves, without the need for a romantic partner and/or children.

Cultivating joy is a skill that can be honed, a choice that can be made, and something that is found in the tiniest of things, from the sound of the dawn chorus or an uplifting song, to a delicious breakfast or a simple walk in nature. Joy is not dependent on anyone or anything in particular, only on our own understanding that it is all around us, all the time.

176

Concluding Thoughts

When Tom Cruise uttered the fateful words 'You complete me' to Renée Zellweger (ironically the actress who played the spinster of all spinsters, Bridget Jones) in the 1996 film *Jerry Maguire*, a generation of women were woefully mislead. Because the truth is that we don't need anyone to 'complete' us.

There is no such thing as an 'other half', a 'better half' or any other state of being that suggests you're only 50 per cent of a person. As Ileana (38, Northern California) told me, 'being single and childfree means that I have the time and space to be my full self. I'm a whole person all on my own, and I don't need a partner. This is what brings me joy and fulfilment – having a very fully formed relationship with a very fully formed person: myself.'

Since becoming single myself, I've been on my own journey of self-development, leading me to conclude, without a shadow of a doubt, that the game of life is nothing to do with finding the other half to your whole. Nope. It turns out that the game of life is an 'inside job'. I know you've heard this expression before, and you're either nodding in agreement or rolling your eyes, but I'd like to give you my take on what this actually means. Not least because it has played a huge part in me reaching a place of contentment and peace as a single, childless woman, and so it might help you, too. You see, it hasn't always been the case that I felt so good about either my singleness or my childlessness. It was only by looking inwards, *not* outwards, that I found the answers to the questions about life I'd been searching for, for so many years. By choosing to do this inner work, instead of attempting to 'fix' my external reality with a boyfriend, a baby or anything else, life got so much better. And I want the same for you.

Here's my take.

When we work on – and upgrade – our *internal* environment, our *external* circumstances change for the better. I really

THRIVE SOLO

do believe it is as simple as that. But it's by no means easy. It all begins with our mindset, because to a great extent our thoughts and our feelings are creating our realities. Everything comes back to the way we are thinking, and until we wrap our heads around this hugely important concept, we will not change the way we feel about ourselves, and we will not change our lives. I firmly believe that being single and childless is not the reason we are unhappy or dissatisfied with our lives, even if we think this is the case. We could just as easily have gotten married, had a couple of kids, and been equally miserable and disenchanted. Because it's not actually about what's going on in your outside world, but almost entirely about what's going on *inside*.

Life is in large part about perception and attention; how you perceive things and where you place your focus. Which is why two people living the exact same life made up of the exact same circumstances – education, family, finances, surroundings – can experience two wildly different realities. An 'internal axiom' that the late, great motivational speaker Wayne Dyer used countless times during his lifetime was: 'Change the way you look at things, and the things you look at change.'[1] If we want to get happy with our single lives, rather than looking for the solution in the latest dating app, we're far better off looking at what's going on between our ears, and what we spend our days thinking about. So ask yourself, 'Where is my attention most of the time?' Because for better or for worse, your thoughts *are* impacting your external reality. And until you address the way that you're thinking, you will fail to see the life you desire manifest into your 3D reality.

Eight Practical Tips

It may interest you to know that I've been embracing all of the below practices for the past five years, and as a result of this,

Concluding Thoughts

the way I feel about myself, life and the world has transformed for the better. So settle in and get ready for a pep talk of sorts. Short and sweet. Or perhaps more firm but fair. I'll let you be the judge of that.

1) Pay attention to your thoughts.

Ultimately, it all starts with an awareness of our thoughts. This isn't a new concept, and whether you're into the woo woo or not, it's what multiple great philosophers and thinkers have been trying to tell us for centuries. But for some reason we still don't grasp how incredibly important our thoughts are when it comes to how our lives look. Earl Nightingale told us that we become what we think about most of the time; Marcus Aurelius wrote that the happiness of our life depends upon the quality of our thoughts; Ralph Waldo Emerson said that a man is what he thinks about all day long; and William James told us that the greatest discovery of his generation was that human beings can alter their lives by altering their attitudes of mind.

The power of the mind is real, people, so if your life doesn't look or feel how you'd like it to look and feel, start by paying attention to what's going on between your ears. What you focus on expands, so notice those negative thought patterns and make sure that your dominant thoughts look less like 'Ugh, being single sucks. I'm miserable' and more like 'There are so many wonderful things about being single and I'm choosing to lean into them.' We have to be vigilant when it comes to our thoughts. Period.

THRIVE SOLO

> ## —Top Tip 1—
>
> When you notice a negative thought, simply choose to replace it with a slightly less negative one. You don't have to go straight from 'I'm a worthless loser' to 'I'm winning at life.' You could at first try replacing it with something like 'I'm working on my self-worth' instead.

2) Change the record.

More often than not, *we* are the only ones holding ourselves back from the things that we truly want in life. And this is largely thanks to the limiting beliefs we all hold on to so tightly – most of which we did not choose and are not serving us. You know those stories we tell ourselves, like 'I'm never going to be able to [insert dream here]' or 'It's never going to work' or 'people like me don't become successful' or 'I need a boyfriend and a baby in order to be happy.' We've been playing these records on repeat for so long that we're completely oblivious to the detrimental impact that they're having on our potentially awesome lives. So accustomed have we become to the furious thrash metal and aggressive vocals of Megadeth drilling into our brains 24/7, we have no idea how our lives would change if only we would just throw on some Stevie Wonder.

We have to change the stories we're telling ourselves, because it's those beliefs that are driving our thoughts, those thoughts that are driving our actions, and those actions that are giving us the same old results, time and time again. I would encourage you to have a look at some of the beliefs that might be holding you back from the life that you truly desire. Once you've unearthed them, you can literally choose the beliefs that are going to serve you and get you to where you actually want to go.

Concluding Thoughts

> **—Top Tip 2—**
>
> Record some affirmations beginning with 'I am' on your phone and listen to them every morning just after you wake up. For example: 'I am more than capable of doing X, Y, Z', 'I am worthy and deserving of happiness' and 'I am enough without a partner.'

3) Pay attention to what you are consuming.

This one is also huge. It is vital that you take stock of what you're consuming on a daily basis if you want to improve your life. And no, I'm not talking about whether you're consuming fizzy drinks or electrolyte-filled water, I'm talking about the content that you're allowing into your brain in the form of TV, news, podcasts, social media and (the big one) people. Most of us are blissfully unaware of the enormous impact that the things and people we're allowing access to our minds are having on how we both think and feel.

Here are a few examples:

- **Social media:** Who are you following and what are they populating your feed with? If you feel like you want to curl up in a ball and stuff your face with Doritos every time you come off Instagram, may I suggest having a bit of a cull? If you're unhappily single and childless, for the love of god unfollow those accounts who are constantly posting pictures of their perfect families and replace them with single women who are rocking life. It's not rocket science, but it makes a huge difference.

THRIVE SOLO

- **The news:** I'm not suggesting that you move to a mountain in the Himalayas and leave your phone at base camp, but please, please, please limit your consumption of the news. Of course we need to be across what's happening in the world, but watching three hours of such depressing content that you want to surgically remove your eyeballs with a teaspoon is not helping you, or anyone else for that matter. We don't realise how much of a negative impact overconsumption of the news is having on us.

- **People:** There's a saying that we become the average of the five people we spend the most time with. So, take a look around you, because whoever you're conversing with on a regular basis is impacting your mindset – and your life – for good or for bad. What about that friend who is constantly bitching and moaning? Or the work bestie who unwittingly makes you feel like crap about being single? Or maybe it's your mum whose negativity always leaves you feeling depleted. I'm not suggesting we dump all of our friends and family, but it's worth being more mindful about how the people around you are making you feel. Minimise the time you spend with those who drag you down, and maximise the time you spend with those who inspire and motivate you to grow.

The people and content you allow into your mind are paramount when it comes to your mindset, so it's time to get ruthless. Unfollow accounts and people that drag you down, and replace them with more inspirational accounts, uplifting podcasts and positive people. Then watch how much brighter you feel.

Concluding Thoughts

> **— Top Tip 3—**
>
> Replace the morning news with an inspirational podcast as you get ready for your day.

4) Practice gratitude.

The benefits of cultivating a gratitude practice are, quite frankly, staggering. And if you haven't heard a million wellness gurus waxing lyrical on the subject, then you've clearly been living under a rock in the Outer Hebrides. It's really very simple: gratitude makes us feel better, both physically and mentally. There is also plenty of scientific evidence that shows a relationship between gratitude and well-being, with multiple studies now suggesting that those people who feel more gratitude are far more likely to have higher levels of happiness, as well as significantly lower levels of depression and stress.[2] Plus there is more and more evidence to suggest that gratitude is an important part of mental health and well-being.

With all of these amazing benefits available at our fingertips simply by being thankful for all of the things we're blessed with – and if you're reading this book then you're blessed – wouldn't it be rude not to? For us single, childfree women, hopefully this book has already shown us how much we have to be grateful for; but for those of you not feeling it yet, bringing gratitude into your life will most certainly help you to feel more positive, and will provide a little light relief from those pesky, negative thoughts and feelings. It really is a win–win.

I would suggest you start with a little bit of stationery porn (just me?!) and treat yourself to a beautiful new notebook and pen, or in my case mechanical pencil, and simply write out five things that you feel grateful for. When you begin your day

THRIVE SOLO

by writing down some of the good things in your life, you're starting it off on the right foot. And before you even think about wondering what you have to be grateful for, if it can't be the Adonis watching you as you rise from your slumber, then start with the comfy bed that he's not actually in. Or the roof over your head. Or the fact that you have the ability to walk from the bed to the bathroom (if you do). In other words, it doesn't matter how small you start, just start.

—Top Tip 4—

As you write your list, listen to uplifting music. The research shows that it's not enough to just write down what we're grateful for, we actually have to *feel* it, and even better if we can relate it to a real-life *story* that inspires us. This could be a story involving us, i.e. a stranger helped us out of a sticky situation, and we felt truly grateful, *or* a story in which we witnessed a stranger helping someone else, and we felt the gratitude of that other person — in my experience, music makes it easier to cultivate those feelings.[3]

5) Get up early.

I will never stop talking about this for as long as I live. Cultivating and sticking to a morning routine has been a game-changer for me, and it could be for you too if only you would stop telling yourself that you're 'not a morning person'. Trust me: I wasn't either. I kid you not when I tell you that if you asked my entire family, all of the friends who've known me since school days,

Concluding Thoughts

and all of my ex-boyfriends, not one of them would paint a pretty picture of who I used to be first thing in the morning. So if I can get up early pretty much every day, you can too.

Getting up early and, subsequently, giving yourself the gift of time is a . . . gift. There are no two ways about it. And if you're wondering what the hell you're going to do with the extra time, depending on how long you give yourself, there are any number of things you can do that will ensure you have the best possible day. For starters, you can write out that gratitude list. (Just saying.) You can meditate, journal, go for a run, go for a walk, strength train, do breathwork, start working on that side hustle so you can leave that job you hate. However you decide to spend it, when you create some time and space for yourself at the beginning of the day, rather than rolling out of bed just in time to shower, grab a coffee and rock up at your desk, your life will transform.

And no, it isn't easy. And no, it doesn't feel great in the depths of winter when it's pitch-black and freezing cold outside. And yes, it will take time for your body and mind to adjust. But it is always, always, *always* worth it for the fabulous way that it sets you up for your day (and makes you feel slightly smug). Own your mornings; own your life. The end.

—Top Tip 5—

Get an accountability buddy and take it in turns to call each other. That's how I started, and it's what I still do now.

THRIVE SOLO

6) Get busy getting busy.

One of the best things about being single and not having children is the extra time we have to put towards, well . . . anything we like. There is a whole world out there of cool stuff to learn, do and experience, and we need to make the bloody most of it. When I say 'get busy getting busy', I'm not referring to things like watching Netflix, going for drinks with friends or folding the laundry (not that there's anything wrong with any of them). I'm talking more about getting busy with something that feels purposeful, meaningful or that you love doing so much that you lose all track of time. I'm talking about getting busy doing things that push us outside of our comfort zones so that we can show ourselves what we're truly capable of. I believe that all of us have something that we're here to do, whether we know it or not. And it's our job to work out what it is.

I've also found that having a goal I'm working towards, or a project on the go, drives me forwards in life and gives me a sense of purpose. This is important not just for those of us who are single and without kids, but for everyone. Without purpose in our lives, we're in danger of falling into depression; because the opposite of depression isn't actually happiness, it's purpose. So really ask yourself what you would be doing if time/money/circumstances were no object, and work out how you can start taking baby steps towards it. To quote my favourite line from a poem by Mary Oliver, 'The Summer Day': 'Tell me, what is it you plan to do with your one wild and precious life?' So . . . what?

—Top Tip 6—

Ask yourself: 'What do I enjoy? What am I good at? How do I want to serve the world?' Start there and see where it takes you.

Concluding Thoughts

7) Get out of victimhood.

Forgive me if this one sounds harsh, but some of us really need to hear it. I did. Because it wasn't so long ago that I was a *total* victim. If you find yourself blaming other people, things and circumstances for why your life isn't how you'd like it to be, you might have fallen victim to . . . victimhood. And when we're living our life from that place, we're giving our power away.

You are 100 per cent responsible for your life. No ifs, no buts; it's the truth. I'm not pretending that there aren't plenty of things that can come along and whack us over the head or steer us wildly off course, but it is our responsibility to pick ourselves up, dust ourselves off and keep moving forwards. Once you stop looking outside of yourself for all the reasons why you are where you are, you reclaim your power and you're back in the driver's seat.

—Top Tip 7—

Ask yourself: 'Is there a story that I keep on telling that I need to let go of?' Perhaps you've been telling yourself and anyone who will listen that the reason you're miserable is because you're single. (If so, revisit Tip 2 on changing the record . . .)

---

8) Stop giving a flying fu*k what others think.

I'm finishing strong with possibly *the* biggest thing that holds us back: worrying about the opinions and judgements of others. If I had a dollar for every time I'd let the fear of what a friend/family member/colleague/ex-boyfriend might think stop me from taking action, I'd be a frickin' millionaire by now.

187

THRIVE SOLO

There are 8 billion people in this world. And they're all far too busy worrying about themselves to be worrying about you. No offence.

> ## —Top Tip 8—
>
> Ask yourself: 'What is *actually* going to happen if [insert names here] get together and make fun of me?' The answer in the vast majority of cases is: nothing. So what if they judge? So what if they laugh? Remind yourself that, before long, they'll be moving on to the next thing, and whatever you're doing will be a distant memory.

But don't just take my word for it. Let's hear from a couple of other women whose outer worlds have been positively impacted by doing the inner work.

Karen (51, London), who was always cynical about 'self-help', told me that after reading *The Power of Now* by Eckhart Tolle,[4] she woke up to the fact that 'my life is so much more about my own patterns of thinking than I'd ever realised, and that I have much more control over my life than I'd ever know.' She also said that she'd spent so long feeling like a victim that it hadn't occurred to her that she could actually decide to feel better. For Karen, doing some inner work was a game-changer.

The same goes for Maddie (50, Bristol), for whom her years of being single have been 'a gift'. She has spent a significant amount of time on personal growth, asking herself questions like 'Who am I?', 'What do I want?' and 'What's important to me?' And her conclusion is that 'I think maybe I'm becoming the person I'm supposed to be, actually. There is this strong,

Concluding Thoughts

authentic, creative, cool woman in there who has the space to grow.' Maddie finished by telling me that it's taken her a long time to figure out that there isn't anything holding her back except herself.

Ultimately, happiness is always available to us – it's just a question of choosing it; and putting into practice the above tips is a great start. Drea (38, North East England), who's been single for 10 years, is another who believes that happiness gets to be a choice. In fact, she believes that we can make ourselves miserable, as well as make ourselves happy. She is of the opinion that 'you're in control of your own happiness, but you have to reframe and shift your thoughts, and just keep doing the things that make you happy – you have to make time for it.' She also told me that the key to her happiness is having the wherewithal to pull herself out of the things that are bringing her down, and her process is something she endearingly describes as 'hippo time'. According to Drea, we're all allowed a little 'hippo time', which means 'you can sit and wallow in your little hippo lake' but at some point, you've got to get out of that lake. Drea believes that you can absolutely make yourself happy – 'you just have to choose it.' Fair point, well made.

Step into Your Power

I'd like to leave you with this. As a single woman, you get to live a life that promises just as much joy, meaning, fulfilment, happiness, excitement, hope and peace as any other life on our planet of billions of people (and billions of different stories).

As Kerri (51, Brisbane) says, 'being single is an awesome club to be in.' Karen (51, London) adds that she is living her best life 'not in spite of being single, but because of it'. She says to any single woman out there: 'You already have everything

THRIVE SOLO

that you need for a happy life, inside of YOU.' But only *you* hold the power to go out there and create that life for yourself.

Regardless of what society is telling you, in spite of the expectations of others, and no matter how hard it can feel to be swimming against the tide, it is up to you to embrace and own your single life. You are not defined by your relationship status, and your value is not measured by whether or not you happen to be doing life on your own, or alongside a partner. Do not forget that the negative connotations associated with single women are not based on any kind of innate facts; they are based on narratives and belief systems that were made up long ago by people long since gone. It is up to you to realise this, to let those stories go, and to step fully into your power as a single woman, because your life is as valid as the next person's.

But I also want you to know that you are not alone. There is a whole community of single, childfree women out there who are navigating the same issues as you, who are ready to cheer you along as you go. (And please see p. 193 for more information about my own community, Thrive Solo, or check out my podcast, *Thrive Solo*, wherever you listen to podcasts.)

If you take nothing else from this book, please know this:

You are not a failure.

You are not pitiable.

You are not less than.

There is nothing wrong with you.

You are not too old, too unattractive, too difficult, too weird or too much.

You are no less worthy, no less fabulous and no less interesting than anyone else.

Concluding Thoughts

On the contrary . . .

Your life is enviable.

Your life is peaceful.

Your time is your own.

Your life is freedom-filled.

You have agency and autonomy over your life.

Your emotions and moods are not dependent on the emotions and moods of a partner or a child.

You are afforded the time and space necessary to follow your curiosity, your interests, your passions, your dreams, your desires, and all of the fabulousness this world has to offer.

—

Despite the current worldview of single, childless women, I hope this book has helped you realise that not only is a solo life equally fabulous, meaningful and rewarding as life with a partner and children, but that there are also a whole host of wonderful and underrated perks and advantages that remain overlooked beneath the tsunami of attention directed towards the traditional life path. The stories of the women in this book, along with much of the research I've mentioned, have shown that being single does not inevitably equate to misery and desperation, and nor does being childless automatically equate to loneliness and regret.

For too long, the lives of single women have been misrepresented and falsely portrayed as tales of misery, loneliness and dejection, whereas the well-trodden path of marriage and children has been glorified as a fairy tale with a guaranteed

THRIVE SOLO

happy ending. The disadvantages and downsides of being single and childless have been exaggerated, while the benefits have been disregarded. Meanwhile, the advantages and upsides of family life have been romanticised, while the drawbacks have been glossed over.

But the truth is beginning to make its way out of the shadows, and with it, more and more single women telling the real stories of their lives through articles, books and podcasts. Slowly but surely there is a shift happening, bringing to the surface the realisation – and revelation – that women like us are loving our lives. Sometimes I smile to myself when I think of the changes afoot, and the underworld of thriving, happy singles unapologetically living out their own unique stories. As far as I'm concerned, the world's best-kept secret is that being single and childless is, actually, awesome.

Thrive Solo membership

Thrive Solo is a membership for single women who want to embrace life to the fullest – on their own terms. Whether you already love being single, you're learning to love it, or you're somewhere in between, this community is for you if you're more passionate about building a life you love right now rather than endlessly searching for a relationship.

We connect three times a month on Zoom for uplifting, inspiring live calls. There's also a self_development Book Club, where we dive into one book every two months, alongside exclusive podcast episodes designed to complement each read. Plus, when you join, you'll get immediate access to a treasure trove of past call recordings and extra podcast episodes. And if that wasn't enough, we also host in-person meet-ups at least twice a year in the UK – with hopes of expanding these gatherings as our community grows!

If you're tired of feeling 'less than', wondering if there's something 'wrong' with you, or feeling like you haven't quite 'made it' in life, Thrive Solo is here to change that. You'll be surrounded by a community of brilliant, kind, like-minded single women who will support you, uplift you, and help normalise the solo life. Over time, you'll start to feel more empowered, more confident, and more excited about your journey.

Because life is short, life is precious – and we shouldn't wait for anyone else to start living it fully. Let's Thrive Solo... together.

*Find out more at **www.lucymeggeson.com/thrivesolo** or email me at **lucy@lucymeggeson.com** with any questions.*

ENDNOTES

Introduction

1. United States Census Bureau, 'Unmarried and Single Americans Week: September 17-23, 2023', 17 September 2023. https://www.census.gov/newsroom/stories/unmarried-single-americans-week.html

2. Campbell, Denis, 'Record number of women reach 30 child-free in England and Wales', the *Guardian*, 27 January 2022. https://www.theguardian.com/lifeandstyle/2022/jan/27/women-child-free-30-ons

3. Ministry of Justice , 'Family Court Statistics Quarterly: January to March 2024', 27 June 2024. https://www.gov.uk/government/statistics/family-court-statistics-quarterly-january-to-march-2024/family-court-statistics-quarterly-january-to-march-2024

4. Roseneil, S., Crowhurst, I., Hellesund, T., Santos, A. C. and Stoilova, M., *The Tenacity of the Couple-Norm: Intimate citizen regimes in a changing Europe* (UCL Press, 2020)

5. Levitan, Kathrin, 'Redundancy, the "Surplus Woman" Problem, and the British Census, 1851–1861', *Women's History Review*, *17*(3): 359- 376 (2008). http://digamoo.free.fr/levitan308.pdf

6. Greg, William Rathbone, 'Why Are Women Redundant', *National Review* (1862)

7. 'Superfluous Women.; United Kingdom has 1,179,276 for Whom There Are No Husbands', *New York Times*, 11 August 1912. https://www.nytimes.com/1912/08/11/archives/superfluous-women-united-kingdom-has-1179276-for-whom-there-are-no.html

8. Nicholson, V., *Singled Out* (Penguin, 2008)

THRIVE SOLO

Chapter 1: Freedom

1. Abdur Rahman, A., Veenhoven, R., 'Freedom and Happiness in Nations: A Research Synthesis', *Applied Research Quality Life, 13*: 435–456 (2017). https://doi.org/10.1007/s11482-017-9543-6. Referenced in: Richards, L., 'Research Shows a Link Between Freedom and Happiness', Thrive Global, 23 February 2018. https://community.thriveglobal.com/research-shows-a-link-between-freedom-and-happiness

2. Langer, E. and Rodin, J., 'The effects of choice and enhanced personal responsibility for the aged: A field experiment in an institutional setting', *Journal of Personality and Social Psychology, 34*(2): 191–8 (1976)

3. Campbell, A., *The Sense of Well-Being in America* (McGraw Hill, 1981)

4. Steckermeier, L. C., 'The Value of Autonomy for the Good Life. An Empirical Investigation of Autonomy and Life Satisfaction in Europe', *Social Indicators Research, 154*: 693–723 (2021). https://doi .org/10.1007/s11205-020-02565-8

5. Kislev, E., 'Happiness, Post-Materialist Values, and the Unmarried', *Journal of Happiness Studies* (2017). https://cdn2.psychologytoday.com/assets/happiness_post-materialist_values_and_the_unmarried.pdf

6. Bella DePaulo, *Single at Heart* (Apollo, 2023); Bella DePaulo, *Singled Out* (St Martin's Press, 2006)

Chapter 2: Living Alone

1. Ortiz-Ospina, E., 'Loneliness and Social Collections', Our World in Data, 2020. ourworldindata.org/social-connections-and-loneliness#loneliness-solitude-and-social-isolation

2. Walton, A., 'Are You More Stressed at Home Than at Work? You're Not Alone.', *Forbes*, 23 May 2014. https://www.forbes.com/sites/alicegwalton/2014/05/23/are-you-more-stressed-at-home-than-at-work-youre-not-alone/?sh=13cf683219ea

3. Schulte, B., 'Stress levels higher at home than work for those balancing career and family', *The Guardian*, 31 May 2014. https://www.theguardian.com/society/2014/may/31/more-stress-at-home-than-work

4. Lindberg, S., 'How Does Your Environment Affect Your Mental Health?', *VeryWell*, 23 March 2023. https://www.verywellmind.com/how-your-environment-affects-your-mental-health-5093687

Endnotes

5. Silva, L., 'The Mental Health Benefits of a Clean Home', *Forbes*, 1 December 2022. https://www.forbes.com/health/mind/mental-health-clean-home/; Kolmac Integrated Behavioral Health, 'How Your Home Environment Affects Your Mental Health', 1 July 2020. https://www.kolmac.com/how-your-home-environment-affects-your-mental-health/

6. Saxbe, D. E. and Repetti, R., 'No Place Like Home: Home Tours Correlate with Daily Patterns of Mood and Cortisol', *Personality and Social Psychology Bulletin, 36*(1) (2009). https://journals.sagepub.com/doi/10.1177/0146167209352864

Chapter 3: Solitude

1. Nguyen, T., 'The importance of solitude – why time on your own can sometimes be good for you', 28 April 2023. https://www.durham.ac.uk/research/current/thought-leadership/2023/04/the-importance-of-solitude--why-time-on-your-own-can-sometimes-be-good-for-you/

2. Long, C. R. and Averill, J. R., 'Solitude: An Exploration of Benefits of Being Alone', *Journal for the Theory of Social Behaviour, 33*(1): 21-44 (5 March 2003). https://www.researchgate.net/publication/227867774_Solitude_An_Exploration_of_Benefits_of_Being_Alone

3. Maitland, S., *How to Be Alone* (The School of Life, 3) (Macmillan, 2014)

4. Storr, A., *Solitude: A Return to the Self* (The Free Press, 1988)

5. Maslow, A., *Motivation and Personality* (Harper & Brothers, 1954)

6. Weinstein et al., "Balance between solitude and socializing: everyday solitude time both benefits and harms well-being," *Scientific Reports* https://doi.org/10.1038/s41598-023-44507-7

7. Weinstein, N., Hansen, H. and Nguyen, T., *Solitude: The Science and Power of Being Alone* (Cambridge University Press, 2024); Holly Pascoe, From the Authors; Solitude with, Netta Weinstein, Heather Hanson & Thuy-vy T. Nguyen, https://www.cambridge.org/core/blog/2024/03/20/solitude-with-netta-weinstein-heather-hanson-amp-thuy-vy-t-nguyen/

8. Weinstein, N., Hansen, H. and Nguyen, T., 'Who feels good in solitude? A qualitative analysis of the personality and mindset factors relating to well-being when alone', *European Journal of Social Psychology*: 1–15 (2023). https://doi.org/10.1002/ejsp.2983

9. Maitland, S., *How to Be Alone*

THRIVE SOLO

10. Ermer, A. E., Proulx, C. M. 'Associations Between Social Connectedness, Emotional Well-Being, and Self-Rated Health Among Older Adults: Difference by Relationship Status', *Res Aging*. 2019 Apr;41(4):336-361. doi: 10.1177/0164027518815260. Epub 2018 Nov 28. PMID: 30486747.

11. Sarton, M., *Journal of a Solitude* (W.W. Norton & Co., 1993)

12. Hoan, E. and MacDonald, G., 'Personality and Well-Being Across and Within Relationship Status', *Personality and Social Psychology Bulletin, 0*(0) (2024). https://doi.org/10.1177/01461672231225571

13. Rauch, J., 'Caring for Your Introvert', *The Atlantic*, March 2003. https://www.theatlantic.com/magazine/archive/2003/03/caring-for-your-introvert/302696/

Chapter 4: Careers and Financial Independence

1. Williams, A., 'Workingmums Survey: Full Results 2022', Workingmums, 2022. https://www.workingmums.co.uk/workingmums-survey-full-results-2022/

2. Fawcett Society, 'Paths to Parenthood: Uplifting new mothers at work', 6 November 2023. https://www.fawcettsociety.org.uk/paths-to-parenthood-uplifting-new-mothers-at-work

3. 'How Motherhood Hurts Careers', 30 January 2024. https://www.economist.com/interactive/graphic-detail/2024/01/30/how-motherhood-hurts-careers

4. Monro, K. *Losing It: How We Popped Our Cherry over the Last 80 Years* (Icon Books, 2013); Monro, K. *The First Time: True Tales of Virginity Lost & Found* (Icon Books, 2011)

5. Slater and Gordon, 'Money worries are a top reason why people split', 8 January 2018. https://www.slatergordon.co.uk/newsroom/money-worries-top-list-of-reasons-why-couples-will-split-in-2018/

6. Institute for Divorce Financial Analysts, 'Survey: Certified Divorce Financial Analyst® (CDFA®) Professionals Reveal the Leading Causes of Divorce'. https://institutedfa.com/leading-causes-divorce/

Endnotes

Chapter 5: Solo Travel

1. Bianchi, C., 'Solo Holiday Travellers: Motivators and Drivers of Satisfaction and Dissatisfaction', *International Journal of Tourism Research,18*(2): 197-208 (22 May 2015). https://www.researchgate.net/publication/277024827_Solo_Holiday_Travellers_Motivators_and_Drivers_of_Satisfaction_and_Dissatisfaction_Solo_Holiday_Travellers; Teng, Y. M., Wu, K. S. and Lee, Y. C., 'Do personal values and motivation affect women's solo travel intentions in Taiwan?', *Humanities & Social Sciences Communications, 10*(8) (2023). https://doi.org/10.1057/s41599-022-01499-5; Condor, 'Explore Solo Travel Trends & Stats by Demographics, Destination, Industry & Why Solo Travel Continues to Rise!'. https://www.condorferries.co.uk/solo-travel-statistics; Solo Traveller, 'Solo Travel Statistics, Data 2023 – 2024: Historical Trends, Sources Cited'. https://solotravelerworld.com/about/solo-travel-statistics-data/; Keenan, S., 'Why more of us are travelling solo', WTM Global Hub, 3 August 2022. https://hub.wtm.com/blog/adventure/why-more-of-us-are-travelling-solo/

2. Ling Yang, E. C., 'What motivates and hinders people from travelling alone? A study of solo and non-solo travellers', *Current Issues in Tourism, 24*(3):1-14 (2010). https://www.researchgate.net/publication/346452536_What_motivates_and_hinders_people_from_travelling_alone_A_study_of_solo_and_non-solo_travellers

Chapter 6: Not Having Kids

1. 'Regretful Parents,' https://www.reddit.com/r/regretfulparents/

2. Quoted in Otte, J., 'Love and regret: mothers who wish they'd never had children,' *The Guardian*, 9 May 2016. https://www.theguardian.com/lifeandstyle/2016/may/09/love-regret-mothers-wish-never-had-children-motherhood

3. From *Barbie* (2023), [film] Dir. Greta Gerwig, USA: Warner Bros.

4. Donath, O., 'Regretting Motherhood: A Sociopolitical Analysis', *Journal of Women in Culture and Society, 40*(2) (2015). https://www.academia.edu/9820246/Regretting_Motherhood_A_Sociopolitical_Analysis

5. Quoted in Jayson, S., 'Are parents happier? Dads may be, but not moms, singles', *USA Today*, 15 January 2013. https://eu.usatoday.com/story/news/nation/2013/01/15/parents-childless-happiness-research/1830429/

THRIVE SOLO

6. Quoted in Jayson, S., 'Are parents happier? Dads may be, but not moms, singles', *USA Today*, 15 January 2013. https://eu.usatoday.com/story/news/nation/2013/01/15/parents-childless-happiness-research/1830429/

7. Gov.uk, 'Parental rights and responsibilities'. https://www.gov.uk/parental-rights-responsibilities

8. The Children's Society, 'Children's mental health statistics'. https://www.childrenssociety.org.uk/what-we-do/our-work/well-being/mental-health-statistics

9. Australian Psychological Society, 'Children 18 months to 18 years showing serious mental health issues, APS survey reveals', 27 November 2022. https://psychology.org.au/about-us/news-and-media/media-releases/2022/children-18-months-to-18-years-showing-serious-men

10. Bailey, A., 'Miley Cyrus Says Climate Change Has Affected Her Stance on Having Kids', *Elle*, 13 July 2019. https://www.elle.com/culture/celebrities/a28381501/miley-cyrus-climate-change-baby-plans-liam-hemsworth/

11. Ibbetson, C., 'Why do people choose to not have children?', YouGov, 9 January 2020. https://yougov.co.uk/society/articles/25364-why-are-britons-choosing-not-have-children

12. Quoted in Wills, K., 'Meet the Londoners staying childless to save the planet', the *Standard*, 15 July 2020. https://www.standard.co.uk/lifestyle/parenthood-not-having-children-for-environment-planet-eco-a4390541.html

13. Hunt, E., 'BirthStrikers: meet the women who refuse to have children until climate change ends', *The Guardian*, 12 March 2019. https://www.theguardian.com/lifeandstyle/2019/mar/12/birthstrikers-meet-the-women-who-refuse-to-have-children-until-climate-change-ends

Chapter 7: Sex

1. Morales-Brown, P., 'Does sex provide health benefits?', *Medical News Today*, 22 November 2023. https://www.medicalnewstoday.com/articles/316954?c=598121379108

2. Center for Women's Health, 'The Benefits of a Healthy Sex Life'. https://www.ohsu.edu/womens-health/benefits-healthy-sex-life

Endnotes

3. Wellings, K., Palmer, M. J., Machiyama, K. and Slaymaker, E., 'Changes in, and factors associated with, frequency of sex in Britain: evidence from three National Surveys of Sexual Attitudes and Lifestyles (Natsal)', *The BMJ*, 365:l1525 (2019). https://www.bmj.com/content/365/bmj.l1525

4. Nolsoe, E., 'How much sex are Britons having?' YouGov, 24 February 2020. https://yougov.co.uk/society/articles/27850-how-much-sex-are-britons-having

5. Herbenick, D., Rosenberg, M., Golzarri-Arroyo, L. *et al.*, 'Changes in Penile-Vaginal Intercourse Frequency and Sexual Repertoire from 2009 to 2018: Findings from the National Survey of Sexual Health and Behavior', *Archives of Sexual Behavior, 51*: 1419-1433 (2022). https://doi.org/10.1007/s10508-021-02125-2

6. Hill, N. *Outwitting the Devil: The Secret to Freedom and Success* (Sterling Publishing, 2011 [1938])

7. Baumeister, R. F., Catanese, K. R. and Vohs, K. D., 'Is There a Gender Difference in Strength of Sex Drive? Theoretical Views, Conceptual Distinctions, and a Review of Relevant Evidence', *Personality and Social Psychology Review, 5*(3): 242-273 (2001). https://doi.org/10.1207/S15327957PSPR0503_5

8. Shaw, G., 'Sex Drive: How Do Men and Women Compare?', WebMD, 27 March 2024. https://www.webmd.com/sex/features/sex-drive-how-do-men-women-compare

9. Brotto, L. A. (2010). The DSM diagnostic criteria for hypoactive sexual desire disorder in men. *Journal of Sex Medicine*, 7, 2015-2030. doi: 10.1111/j.1743-6109.2010.01860.x

10. Sarrel, P. M., 'Sexuality and menopause', *Obstetrics & Gynecology, 75*(4 Suppl):26S-30S (1990); discussion 31S-35S. PMID: 2179787. https://pubmed.ncbi.nlm.nih.gov/2179787/

11. Nall, R., 'How does menopause affect sex drive?', *Medical News Today*, 6 March 2023. https://www.medicalnewstoday.com/articles/320266#what-is-the-link

12. Power, M. *Love Me! One Woman's Search for a Different Happy Ever After* (Picador, 2024)

13. According to a comprehensive survey of the sex lives of Americans: Henley, J., 'American reveals its sexual secrets', *The Guardian,* 5 October 2010. https://www.theguardian.com/lifeandstyle/2010/oct/05/sex-us-american-attitudes-survey

THRIVE SOLO

14. Broster, A., 'What Are the Health Benefits of Female Masturbation?', *Forbes*, 22 June 2020. https://www.forbes.com/sites/alicebroster/2020/06/22/what-are-the-health-benefits-of-female-masturbation/

15. Cleveland Clinic, 'Masturbation', 25 October 2022. https://my.clevelandclinic.org/health/articles/24332-masturbation; Mintz, L., 'A Touchy Subject: The Health Benefits of Masturbation, *Psychology Today,* 28 January 2014. https://www.psychologytoday.com/gb/blog/stress-and-sex/201401/touchy-subject-the-health-benefits-masturbation

16. Gloria Brame quoted in Broster, A., 'What Are the Health Benefits of Female Masturbation?', *Forbes,* 22 June 2020. https://www.forbes.com/sites/alicebroster/2020/06/22/what-are-the-health-benefits-of-female-masturbation/

17. 'The UK's Sex Toy Habits Revealed!, *Idealo,* 23 August 2023. https://www.idealo.co.uk/magazine/lifestyle-leisure/uk-sex-toys-habits

18. 'Size of the sex toy market worldwide from 2016 to 2030', March 2022. https://www.statista.com/statistics/587109/size-of-the-global-sex-toy-market/

Chapter 8: Friendships and Other Relationships

1. Aristotle, *The Nicomachean Ethics*

2. Choi, K. W. *et al.*, 'An Exposure-Wide and Mendelian Randomization Approach to Identifying Modifiable Factors for the Prevention of Depression', *American Journal of Psychiatry, 177*(10) (October 2020). https://psychiatryonline.org/doi/10.1176/appi.ajp.2020.19111158

3. Pezirkianidis, C., Galanaki, E., Raftopoulou, G., Moraitou, D., Stalikas, A., 'Adult friendship and wellbeing: A systematic review with practical implications', *Frontiers in Psychology*, 14:1059057 (24 January 2023). https://www.ncbi.nlm.nih.gov/pmc/articles/PMC9902704/

4. Traister, R., *All the Single Ladies* (Simon & Schuster, 2016)

5. Cohen, R. *The Other Significant Others* (St Martin's Press, 2024)

6. Cohen, R., 'What if Friendship, Not Marriage, Was at the Center of Life?', *The Atlantic*, 20 October 2020. https://www.theatlantic.com/family/archive/2020/10/people-who-prioritize-friendship-over-romance/616779/

Endnotes

7. Sarkisian, N., and Gerstel, N., 'Does singlehood isolate or integrate? Examining the link between marital status and ties to kin, friends, and neighbors', *Journal of Social and Personal Relationships, 33*(3) (August 2015). https://www.researchgate.net/publication/281539387_Does_singlehood_isolate_or_integrate_Examining_the_link_between_marital_status_and_ties_to_kin_friends_and_neighbors

8. Musick, K., and Bumpass, L., 'Re-Examining the Case for Marriage: Union Formation and Changes in Well-Being', *Journal of Marriage and Family,74*(1):1-18 (1 February 2012). https://pmc.ncbi.nlm.nih.gov/articles/PMC3352182/

9. Barrett, M., and McIntosh, M. *The Anti-Social Family* (Verso, 1982)

Closing Thoughts and Eight Practical Tips

1. 'Change the way you look at things, and the things you look at change.': https://www.drwaynedyer.com/blog/tag/the-way-you-look-at-things/#:~:text=The%20truth%20of%20this%20little,a%20particle%20changes%20the%20particle.

2. Seligman, M.E., Steen, T.A., Park, N. and Peterson, C., 'Positive psychology progress: empirical validation of interventions', *American Psychologist, 60*(5):410-21 (Jul–Aug 2005). https://pubmed.ncbi.nlm.nih.gov/16045394/

3. The Huberman Lab, 'The Science of Gratitude & How to Build a Gratitude Practice', 21 November 2021. https://www.hubermanlab.com/episode/the-science-of-gratitude-and-how-to-build-a-gratitude-practice

4. Tolle, E. *The Power of Now* (Namaste Publishing, 1997)

ACKNOWLEDGMENTS

My mum, Sue, for always taking the time to ask me about the book during the period I spent writing in Dorset – I love you.

My brother, Ben, and my sister, Annie, who were so incredibly encouraging and supportive throughout the process of writing this book. I don't know where I would be without you and I love you both more than you know.

Flash, Blue, Moss & Wolfie – I may not have kids, but being an auntie to the four of you is one of the greatest joys of my life. I hope you know how much I adore you all. Blue, you might have to force the boys to read this book!

My brand new nephew, Ruben, you're brand new to this world as I write this, and I've only met you once, but I can't wait to get to know you and watch you grow – thanks for coming along so that I can have cuddles when the others don't want them so much anymore!

My friend, Claire, who cried when I told her about my book deal, and who has been beyond encouraging and kind throughout the whole process – may we always laugh at how amusing we are on our walks by the river. And to my other close friends – I'm sorry for being such an absent friend over the last couple of years whilst juggling the podcast and the book – you guys are family which is how I know I can get away with it!

My agent, Kate, thank you for believing in me and this book, and for all your help and guidance.

To the team at Bloomsbury: thank you for giving me a book deal and making this book a reality. But special thanks to my editor, Holly, without whom this book wouldn't exist at all. Thank you for reaching out to me in the first place, and for being such a wonderful editor. I couldn't have done this without you.

And to the team at Hay House: thank you for taking this book to the US! I'm so grateful to be working with you all. Special thanks to Amy Kiberd for coming up with the name for the UK version of the book, *Shiny Happy Singles*!

A special mention to my cat, Johnny, who throughout the very solitary process of writing this book has been by my side literally every step of the way; and whose little face and general adorableness have brought me back down to earth in my moments of panic and overwhelm. You are not 'just a cat' – you are the one and only being who has been with me as I wrote every single word of this book, and your presence continues to bring me a sense of peace and joy that cannot be overstated. I am so grateful for the connection we share. Thank you for coming into my life.

Finally, thank you to . . . me. You never in a million years thought you would write a book. It was never on your list of goals – you were always more driven to write an album! I'm proud of you for knuckling down, keeping on keeping on, especially in the moments where it felt really, really hard. Writing a book has been more arduous than you ever could have imagined, but you bloody did it. I hope you know your own worth; I hope you're beginning to understand that you are just as capable as anyone else, despite all of the self-doubt. Keep striving to fulfil all of the potential you know that you have inside you. You've got this.

ABOUT THE AUTHOR

Lucy Meggeson is a former BBC *Radio 2* producer and host of the *Thrive Solo* podcast. She's a regular on Jo Good's BBC Radio London show and has been a guest on various other radio and podcasts, including Jeremy Vine's BBC *Radio 2* show and Peter McGraw's *Solo: The Single Person's Guide to a Remarkable Life*. Lucy is based in London. She's childfree and has been single for over seven years. She lives alone and enjoys a full, peaceful, contented, and meaningful life (with her cat).

www.lucymeggeson.com

Hay House Titles of Related Interest

YOU CAN HEAL YOUR LIFE, the movie,
starring Louise Hay & Friends
(available as an online streaming video)
www.hayhouse.com/louise-movie

THE SHIFT, the movie,
starring Dr. Wayne W. Dyer
(available as an online streaming video)
www.hayhouse.com/the-shift-movie

---

*F THE SHOULDS. DO THE WANTS.: Get Clear on Who You Are,
What You Want, and Why You Want It* by Tricia Huffman

*THE PROMISE: Break Free from Limitation and Reclaim
Your Inner Power* by Mandy Morris

*PROTECT YOUR PEACE: Nine Unapologetic Principles for
Thriving in a Chaotic World* by Trent Shelton

*THE QUEEN'S PATH: A Revolutionary Guide to Women's Empowerment
and Sovereignty* by Stacey Simmons, Ph.D.

All of the above are available at your local bookstore, or may be ordered
by contacting Hay House (see next page).

We hope you enjoyed this Hay House book. If you'd like to receive our online catalog featuring additional information on Hay House books and products, or if you'd like to find out more about the Hay Foundation, please contact:

Hay House LLC, P.O. Box 5100, Carlsbad, CA 92018-5100
(760) 431-7695 or (800) 654-5126
www.hayhouse.com® • www.hayfoundation.org

Published in Australia by:
Hay House Australia Publishing Pty Ltd
18/36 Ralph St., Alexandria NSW 2015
Phone: +61 (02) 9669 4299
www.hayhouse.com.au

Published in the United Kingdom by:
Hay House UK Ltd
1st Floor, Crawford Corner,
91–93 Baker Street, London W1U 6QQ
Phone: +44 (0)20 3927 7290
www.hayhouse.co.uk

Published in India by:
Hay House Publishers (India) Pvt Ltd
Muskaan Complex, Plot No. 3,
B-2, Vasant Kunj, New Delhi 110 070
Phone: +91 11 41761620
www.hayhouse.co.in

Let Your Soul Grow

Experience life-changing transformation—one video at a time—with guidance from the world's leading experts.

www.healyourlifeplus.com

Join the Hay House E-mail Community, Your Ultimate Resource for Inspiration

Stay inspired on your journey—Hay House is here to support and empower you every step of the way!

Sign up for our **Present Moments Newsletter** to receive weekly wisdom and reflections directly from Hay House CEO Reid Tracy. Each message offers a unique perspective, grounded in Reid's decades of experience with Hay House and the publishing industry.

As a member of our e-mail community, you'll enjoy these benefits:

- **Inspiring Insights:** Discover new perspectives and expand your personal transformation with content, tips, and tools that will uplift, motivate, and inspire.
- **Exclusive Access:** Connect with world-renowned authors and experts on topics that support your journey of self-discovery and spiritual enrichment.
- **Early Updates:** Get the latest information on new and best-selling books, audiobooks, card decks, online courses, events, and more.
- **Special Offers:** Enjoy periodic announcements about discounts, limited-time offers, and giveaways.
- **Ongoing Savings:** Receive 20% off virtually all products in our online store, all day, every day, as long as you're a newsletter subscriber.

Don't miss out on this opportunity to elevate your journey with Hay House! **Sign Up Now!**

Visit **www.hayhouse.com/newsletters** to sign up today!

MEDITATE.
VISUALIZE.
LEARN.

With the **Empower You**
Unlimited Audio *Mobile App*

Unlimited access to the entire Hay House audio library!

You'll get:

- 600+ inspiring and life-changing **audiobooks**
- 1,000+ ad-free **guided meditations** for sleep, healing, relaxation, spiritual connection, and more
- Hundreds of audios **under 20 minutes** to easily fit into your day
- **Exclusive content** *only* for subscribers
- **New audios** added every week
- No credits, **no limits**

Listen to the audio version of this book for FREE!

★★★★★ **Life changing.**
"My fav app on my entire phone, hands down! – Gigi"

Scan me with your phone camera!

TRY FOR FREE!
Go to: hayhouse.com/listen-free